Oriens

ORIENS

A Pilgrimage Through Advent and Christmas

November 29, 2020–February 2, 2021

FR. JOEL SEMBER

Our Sunday Visitor
Huntington, Indiana

Copyright © 2020 by Fr. Joel Sember

25 24 23 22 21 20   1 2 3 4 5 6 7 8 9

All rights reserved. With the exception of short excerpts for critical reviews, no part of this work may be reproduced or transmitted in any form or by any means whatsoever without permission from the publisher. For more information, visit: www.osv.com/permissions.

Our Sunday Visitor Publishing Division
Our Sunday Visitor, Inc.
200 Noll Plaza
Huntington, IN 46750
www.osv.com
1-800-348-2440

ISBN: 978-1-68192-659-9 (Inventory No. T2518)
1. RELIGION—Holidays—Christmas & Advent.
2. RELIGION—Christian Living—Prayer.
3. RELIGION—Christianity—Catholic.
eISBN: 978-1-68192-660-5
LCCN: 2020935643

Cover design: Tyler Ottinger
Cover art: Adobe Stock
Interior design: Amanda Falk

PRINTED IN THE UNITED STATES OF AMERICA

Dedicated to the Queen of Heaven
in gratitude for her visit to Champion, Wisconsin,
on October 9, 1859

+

and to Tim Schiebe,
my first pilgrim partner

+

and to all my fellow pilgrims,
who have walked with me
on the way

+

¡Buen Camino!

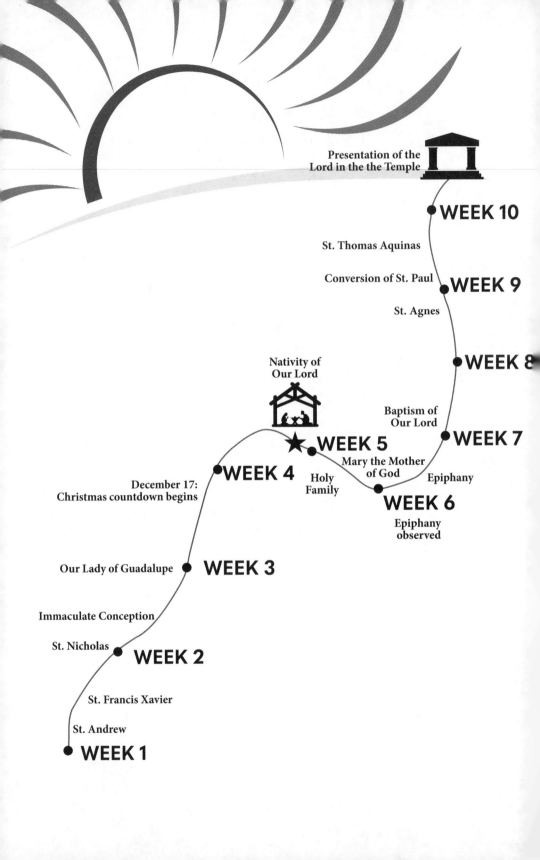

Presentation of the
Lord in the the Temple

WEEK 10

St. Thomas Aquinas

Conversion of St. Paul

WEEK 9

St. Agnes

WEEK 8

Nativity of
Our Lord

Baptism of
Our Lord

WEEK 7

WEEK 5

Mary the Mother
of God

Epiphany

December 17:
Christmas countdown begins

WEEK 4

Holy
Family

WEEK 6

Epiphany
observed

Our Lady of Guadalupe

WEEK 3

Immaculate Conception

St. Nicholas

WEEK 2

St. Francis Xavier

St. Andrew

WEEK 1

Contents

Introduction

Give a man a fish, you feed him for a day.
Teach a man to pray, and you feed him for a lifetime.

TEACH A MAN TO PRAY ...

There are many wonderful Advent books full of moving meditations. This isn't one of them. Instead of giving you meditations I came up with, *Oriens* will teach you how to meditate for yourself. If you don't really know how to pray with Scripture, this book will teach you. If you already know how to pray, then it will help you pray better.

I left space each day for you to journal your prayer experiences. When you get to the end of the book, you will find it has become full of moving meditations — not my meditations but yours. I hope that, as you learn to go deeper in your conversations with God, prayer becomes your favorite part of each day and this season takes on a whole new meaning.

"DO YOU WANT TO WALK THE CAMINO WITH ME?"

It was my third year of theology studies at the North American College in Rome. We had two weeks of Easter vacation to go experience Europe. A classmate and I decided to walk the *Camino Portugués*, a short version of the famous medieval pilgrimage route across Spain. (It's so famous that it's called *El Camino*, which simply means "the way" in Spanish.)

I bought some shoes and borrowed a backpack, and we flew to Lisbon. We took a train to the Portuguese border and then spent a week walking to the burial place of Saint James the apostle. Something special happened on the way. I started to see myself, and the ordinary world, in a whole new way. And I fell in love with walking pilgrimages.

Three years later, I was back in America as a newly ordained priest. "We don't have to fly to Europe to walk down the road," I thought. I scoped out a walking route to a local shrine, lined up places to stay every twelve miles or so, and found people to bring us food each night. Twenty-two people joined me on the pilgrimage. Their lives were changed, and I became hooked on pilgrimages.

Every year for the past ten years, I've led a five-day walking pilgrimage to the Shrine of Our Lady of Good Help in Champion, Wisconsin. I never cease to come away with some new gift, blessing, or lesson learned on the way.

A walking pilgrimage is a much different experience from a bus pilgrimage. When you ride a bus to a shrine, it's mostly about the destination. Pilgrims look forward to a big "Aha" moment when they arrive. Walking pilgrims, on the other hand, learn the joy of the journey. They see familiar roads in a whole new way. They appreciate the beauty around them. They enter into the ebb and flow of nature. They draw closer to the people they walk with. They learn to keep their eyes open for encounters with God along the way. Most of all, they learn to put one foot in front of the other and keep walking no matter what.

A walking pilgrimage is about more than the destination; it's a journey of the heart. It changes you in ways you never expected.

THE ADVENT JOURNEY

So what does this have to do with Advent? We all struggle with Advent. The Church is telling us to slow down, but the world is telling us, "Hurry up." We rush around preparing for the birth of Jesus. We look forward to the big "Aha" moment waiting for us at Christmas. And we always seem to miss out somehow. How is it that every year Christmas seems less merry and bright than we were hoping it would be?

The problem is that we keep treating Advent like the busy bus on the way to Christmas. We expect to step off at Bethlehem and have some kind of amazing experience. Yet Holy Mother Church designed Advent to be more like a walking pilgrimage. You take a little step every day. If you're open to it, you learn to enjoy the journey. You connect with the people around you. You enter into a new rhythm. The ordinary things of life take on a new meaning. God meets you on the road.

Think of this book as a *Camino* guide. It will show you how to step off the Christmas bus and walk the Advent road one day at a time. You will learn that Advent and Christmas are more than destinations; they involve a journey of the heart.

KEEP WALKING

This book covers nearly ten weeks, from the first Sunday of Advent on November 29 to the Feast of the Presentation on February 2. Why does it go so long? It is set up to let us spend four weeks preparing and forty days celebrating Christmas (kind of like the forty days of Lent followed by the fifty days of Easter).

We need those extra days. None of the people who saw the Christ Child in person understood the true meaning of Christmas. It was only in the days and years afterward that the "dawn from on high" began to rise in their hearts (Lk 1:78, Lectionary). The same is true for us in our ongoing journey of faith. Maintaining this devotional until February 2 will help us continue to see Jesus in the ordinary. Besides, it's easier to find time to pray in the post-Christmas lull, and we need a little help getting through the low time in January.

You don't have to walk the whole way with me; it's your journey, and you can quit anytime. But let me encourage you to plan for the long walk.

Consider putting up your Christmas tree a little later this year. Put on the lights and ornaments, but don't plug in the lights until the Light of the World is born on December 25. Then keep your tree lit all through the twelve days until January 6. Plan to keep at least your Advent wreath and Nativity scene up until February 2, the Feast of the Presentation (also known as Candlemas).

This *Oriens* journey may seem now like a long one, but you'll be surprised at how quickly it passes. And you'll really enjoy those extra days.

IF YOU MISS A DAY

Even when you are too busy to pray, try to at least open this book and read the Scripture passage each day. If you end up missing a day or two (or even a week), don't try to go back and do all the meditations you missed. Just skip ahead to the current day and pray that one well.

It is not important that you do every single meditation. What matters is that you put your heart into your prayer. Prayer is experiencing how our Father looks at you with love. Holiness is learning to live in his long, loving gaze every moment of your life.

You might assume, because I wrote this book, that I'm great at praying. Far from it!

I was trained as a spiritual director through the Institute for Priestly Formation. I have taught countless numbers of people how to pray. I've been on pilgrimages and retreats and even a thirty-day silent retreat. But the truth is, unless I'm actually on a retreat or a pilgrimage, I usually pray badly. Most days I'm too busy, distracted, self-absorbed, or lazy to really pray well. And the problem is compounded during the busy Advent and Christmas season.

I wrote this book because I need it too! I will be praying with you and for you this whole season. Please pray for me and for your fellow *Oriens* pilgrims. We each make our own journey, and every journey is unique, but no one walks alone. *¡Buen Camino!*

Father Joel Sember
Priest, Pastor, Pilgrim

Suggested Calendar for the Advent and Christmas Season

November 29, First Sunday of Advent: Light the first candle on your Advent wreath.

December 6, Second Sunday of Advent: Light the first and second candles on your Advent wreath. *(Optional: Give some treats for Saint Nicholas Day!)*

December 8 (Tuesday): Solemnity of the Immaculate Conception. Put up your crèche (manger scene).

December 13, Third Sunday of Advent: Light the first, second, and third (rose) candles on your Advent wreath.

Before December 17: Put up your Christmas tree. Decorate it, but don't plug the lights in. Wait until the Light of the World is born.

December 20, Fourth Sunday of Advent: Light all four candles on your Advent wreath.

December 24 or 25: After attending Christmas Mass, put the Baby Jesus in the crèche, and light up your Christmas tree. Change the candles in your Advent wreath to white.

January 1 (Friday): Octave Day of Christmas, Solemnity of Mary, the Holy Mother of God. Start the New Year with Mary.

January 6 (Wednesday): Epiphany. Have a family party to bless your home with blessed chalk. Afterward you can take down the tree (if you want to) and the decorations, but don't put away the Advent wreath or the crèche.

February 2 (Tuesday): Feast of the Presentation. Have one last Christmas party! Light the candles on your wreath, and have a family Candlemas procession to the crèche. Sing Christmas carols. Then put away any remaining Christmas decorations.

Blessing of an Advent Wreath

The use of the Advent wreath is a traditional practice that has found its place in the Church as well as in the home. The blessing of an Advent wreath takes place on the First Sunday of Advent or on the evening before the First Sunday of Advent. When the blessing of the Advent wreath is celebrated in the home, it is appropriate that it be blessed by a parent or another member of the family.

All make the sign of the cross together: + In the Name of the Father, and of the Son, and of the Holy Spirit.
Leader: Our help is in the name of the Lord.
Response: Who made heaven and earth.
Leader: A reading from the book of the prophet Isaiah:

> The people who walked in darkness
>   have seen a great light;
> Upon those who dwelt in the land of gloom
>   a light has shone.
> You have brought them abundant joy
>   and great rejoicing;
> As they rejoice before you as at the harvest,
>   as men make merry when dividing spoils. ...
> For a child is born to us, a son is given us;
>   upon his shoulder dominion rests.
> They name him Wonder-Counselor, God-Hero,
>   Father-Forever, Prince of Peace.
> His dominion is vast
>   and forever peaceful,
> From David's throne, and over his kingdom,
>   which he confirms and sustains.
> By judgment and justice,
>   both now and forever. (Is 9:1-2, 5-6)

Leader: The Word of the Lord.
Response: Thanks be to God.

Leader: Let us pray.

> Lord our God,
> we praise you for your Son, Jesus Christ:
> He is Emmanuel, the hope of the peoples;
> he is the wisdom that teaches and guides us;
> he is the Savior of every nation.
>
> Lord God,
> let your blessing come upon us
> as we light the candles of this wreath.
> May the wreath and its light
> be signs of Christ's promise to bring us salvation.
> May he come quickly and not delay.
>
> We ask this through Christ our Lord.

Response: Amen.

The blessing may conclude with a verse from "O Come, O Come, Emmanuel":

> O come, desire of nations, bind
> in one the hearts of humankind.
> Bid ev'ry sad division cease,
> and be thyself our Prince of peace.
> Rejoice! Rejoice! Emmanuel
> shall come to thee, O Israel.
>
> — From *Book of Blessings*

Week One

Lectio Divina

This first week we will use an ancient prayer form called *lectio divina* (pronounced "LEK-si-o di-VEE-na"). It has four simple steps, known by their Latin names: *lectio* (reading), *meditatio* (meditation), *oratio* (prayer), and *contemplatio* (contemplation). Don't worry about each Latin word. The prayer form is as simple as this: read, think, talk, listen.

We read a passage of Scripture, and lots of thoughts come to our mind: What does this word mean? What is the cultural and historical context? How have scholars interpreted this particular idea? Those aren't bad things to research. Some of those questions can form the *meditatio* part of prayer. But we need to avoid getting stuck in our own heads.

Reading Scripture isn't really prayer if it doesn't turn into a conversation. That is why we read, think about what we have read, talk to God about what we are thinking, and then listen to him.

This fourth step, to listen, guarantees that our prayer won't be a one-sided conversation. Many people find this *contemplatio* to be a difficult step; they worry about whether they are "doing it right" or "if it's really God." Don't try too hard. Just be quiet and receive.

Prayer is not so much about getting something from God as it is about being with God. We use Scripture as a conversation starter, but conversations with God go deeper than words. Don't worry, I'll walk you through it.

Grace of the Week: Each week has a particular theme or focus. The first week will focus on the creation of the world, the plants, the animals, and human beings. The simplest things can be the easiest to forget and the most profound when they are rediscovered. Pray for the grace to wonder anew at the marvel, mystery, and miracle of God's creation.

First Sunday of Advent

MARK 13:33-37

[Jesus said to his disciples:] "Be watchful! Be alert! You do not know when the time will come. It is like a man traveling abroad. He leaves home and places his servants in charge, each with his work, and orders the gatekeeper to be on the watch. Watch, therefore; you do not know when the lord of the house is coming, whether in the evening, or at midnight, or at cockcrow, or in the morning. May he not come suddenly and find you sleeping. What I say to you, I say to all: 'Watch!'"

Today we begin our Advent journey. Let's take time to plan the trip. Look at the calendar, and make some notes about how you can really enjoy Advent and Christmas this year.

You have twenty-seven days until Christmas. But Christmas is not the only stop on our journey. We will stop to enjoy Saint Nicholas Day next Sunday. Immaculate Conception is a holy day of obligation, so plan to attend Mass on Tuesday, December 8. When will you put up your Christmas tree? Try to make it a family event. Whenever you put up your Christmas tree, I encourage you not to light it until after Christmas Mass. When will you put out your Christmas crèche? Take some time to plan these activities in advance.

For now the only things you need to do are put out the Advent wreath and light the first candle. Everything else can happen in time. While you're looking at your calendar, you might want to plan time for baking, sending cards, present wrapping, and quality family time — whatever makes Christmas special for you.

Right now, as the season begins, you might feel a little anxious. It's normal to be anxious during Advent and Christmas. But this year we're doing something about that: not just planning Christmas but planning to pray through Christmas. To make this journey together, you'll need both a time and a place.

When will you pray? I like to pray right when I get up in the morning. Some people like to pray in the quiet of the evening. It may not happen every day exactly as you planned, but if you don't plan it, chances are it won't happen. So plan a time for prayer.

Where will you pray? If you don't already have a prayer room or a prayer corner, make one. It should be free of distractions and full of things that help you focus on God. Plan a place for prayer.

And let's not just plan; let's pray about the plan. For you can be sure that God has a plan for your Advent and Christmas. Open your heart to his plan: "Come, Holy Spirit, enlighten the eyes of my heart."

Journal your thoughts, feelings, and desires for your Christmas pilgrimage. What do you fear? What do you want to get out of this season? What do you most deeply desire? As you reflect on these questions, turn your heart to God. Is there a way God might be tugging on your heart? What is his desire for your journey?

Now be still for a moment; the Lord is here with you.

The most important part of our Advent journey is an attitude of thanksgiving. So thank God for today's prayer time, and close with an Our Father.

Monday of the First Week of Advent

SAINT ANDREW, APOSTLE

Right from the beginning, Andrew is an evangelist. He has just met Jesus, and he immediately goes to find his brother, Simon Peter, to introduce him (see Jn 1:35–42). Andrew is said to have preached the Gospel in Greece, where he suffered martyrdom at Patras. Bound by ropes to an X-shaped cross, he preached to the crowds for two days before expiring.

Saint Andrew is the patron of Greece, Scotland, and Russia. There is a tradition of beginning a Christmas novena on his feast day. Let us ask Saint Andrew to introduce us to Jesus in our prayer time.

Preparation: Come, Holy Spirit, enlighten the eyes of my heart (see Eph 1:18).

Lectio: We begin *in the beginning*, with the creation of the world. The Bible starts by explaining that everything that is comes from God. The details are not as important as trying to get a sense of the majesty and mystery of it all.

Read the passage below, slowly and prayerfully. Picture an ancient patriarch telling this story to his grandchildren as they sit around a campfire. They have heard it many times before, but still they hang on his every word.

GENESIS 1:1–5, 14–19

In the beginning, when God created the heavens and the earth — and the earth was without form or shape, with darkness over the abyss and a mighty wind sweeping over the waters —

Then God said: Let there be light, and there was light. God saw that the light was good. God then sepa-

rated the light from the darkness. God called the light "day," and the darkness he called "night." Evening came, and morning followed — the first day. ...

Then God said: Let there be lights in the dome of the sky, to separate day from night. Let them mark the seasons, the days and the years, and serve as lights in the dome of the sky, to illuminate the earth. And so it happened: God made the two great lights, the greater one to govern the day, and the lesser one to govern the night, and the stars. God set them in the dome of the sky, to illuminate the earth, to govern the day and the night, and to separate the light from the darkness. God saw that it was good. Evening came, and morning followed — the fourth day.

Meditatio: The Bible opens with a scene of a windswept sea in total darkness. The Hebrew word for wind also means "spirit" and "breath." The wind is the spirit or breath of God.

God is here, and he breaks the silence with four simple words: "Let there be light." And so it is. Then God's word becomes physical in the sun, which gives light and life, and in the moon and stars, which light the night. They are visible signs that point to the Creator. What do they say about God? Read the passage again.

Oratio: The word *Oriens* comes from a Latin verb that means "rising," "dawn," and "East." It gives us the English words *Oriental* and *orientation*. We find it in the Canticle of Zechariah: "In the tender compassion of our God, the dawn from on high shall break upon us" (Lk 1:78, Lectionary). It can also mean "rising one," perhaps a veiled reference to Jesus' resurrection.

One of the rich symbols of Advent is the light overcoming the darkness. Our hearts long for more than just physical light: We long for spiritual light. Yet even if prayer feels dark, faith tells us that we are not alone. The Spirit of God is moving here.

Break the silence, and speak to your Maker. What do you want to say to God?

Contemplatio: Open your heart to receive whatever God might want to give you. How is God's light shining on you?

Read the passage very slowly, a third time. Don't sweat this step. Think of it like sensing the direction of the wind or basking for a moment in the sun's light. Contemplation is being in relationship. Be with the God who is always with you, and receive his loving presence with you and for you.

QUESTIONS FOR JOURNALING

1. What was my most noticeable thought, feeling, or desire during prayer time today?
2. Did I notice God's presence in any particular way? If I did, how would I describe that? If not, how did I feel about it?
3. Can I name one area in my life where I want God's light to shine a little more brightly this Advent?

_____

_____

_____

_____

_____

_____

_____

_____

_____

_____

_____

_____

_____

_____

_____

_____

Close with the Saint Andrew Novena Prayer:

> Hail and blessed be the hour and moment in which the Son of God was born of the most pure Virgin Mary, at midnight, in Bethlehem, in the piercing cold. In that hour vouchsafe, I beseech thee, O my God, to hear my prayer and grant my desires, [here mention your requests], through the merits of Our Savior Jesus Christ and of his Blessed Mother. Amen.

December 1 — Tuesday
Tuesday of the First Week of Advent

Preparation: Come, Holy Spirit, enlighten the eyes of my heart.

Lectio: Read the passage slowly and prayerfully.

PSALM 104:1–3, 5, 19–22, 30

Bless the LORD, my soul!
    LORD, my God, you are great indeed!
You are clothed with majesty and splendor,
    robed in light as with a cloak.
You spread out the heavens like a tent;
    setting the beams of your chambers upon the waters.
You make the clouds your chariot;
    traveling on the wings of the wind. ...

You fixed the earth on its foundation,
    so it can never be shaken. ...

You made the moon to mark the seasons,
    the sun that knows the hour of its setting.
You bring darkness and night falls,
    then all the animals of the forest wander about.
Young lions roar for prey;
    they seek their food from God.
When the sun rises, they steal away
    and settle down in their dens. ...

Send forth your spirit, they are created
    and you renew the face of the earth.

Meditatio: The heavens are always above us, yet we rarely notice them.

The times and seasons all speak to us of God's providence.

Many of us had chances to get out in nature over the summer. Recall a time when you marveled at God's handiwork, when his creation really spoke to you. What was it saying? How did you feel?

Oratio: Read the passage again slowly. What does it mean to be surrounded by creation? How does the vastness of the universe strike you? What about the intricacies of trees and forests, hills and valleys?

Speak to God, who is both engineer and artist of all these things. Bless the Lord, my soul!

Contemplatio: Very slowly read the passage again. Open your heart, and let your Creator speak to you. Receive whatever God wants to give you. You are worth more than all creation. Rest quietly for a moment or two in God's loving presence.

QUESTIONS FOR JOURNALING

1. The ancients saw all creation as a cosmic symphony singing God's praises. What part of the symphony most speaks to me? What is it saying about God's glory?
2. I have a part in the symphony too. How am I called to sing along?
3. I left prayer wanting …

Close with a brief conversation giving thanks to God for your prayer today. Then pray an Our Father.

December 2 — Wednesday
Wednesday of the First Week of Advent

Preparation: Come, Holy Spirit, enlighten the eyes of my heart.

Lectio: Read the passage slowly and prayerfully.

GENESIS 1:20–25

Then God said: Let the water teem with an abundance of living creatures, and on the earth let birds fly beneath the dome of the sky. God created the great sea monsters and all kinds of crawling living creatures with which the water teems, and all kinds of winged birds. God saw that it was good, and God blessed them, saying: Be fertile, multiply, and fill the water of the seas; and let the birds multiply on the earth. Evening came, and morning followed — the fifth day.

Then God said: Let the earth bring forth every kind of living creature: tame animals, crawling things, and every kind of wild animal. And so it happened: God made every kind of wild animal, every kind of tame animal, and every kind of thing that crawls on the ground. God saw that it was good.

Meditatio: Are you a dog person or a cat person? Think of the incredible variety of animals: cows and kangaroos, chickadees and elephants. All kinds of fish, from minnow to marlin. Birds that swim and mammals that fly. Lots and lots of insects.

What are some animals that you just love? What animals do you fear or find creepy? God made them all, each and every one. Every animal has a purpose. Let your thoughts and feelings rise to the surface. Read the passage again slowly.

Oratio: Turn to God, and speak to him about what is on your mind and in your heart. When you are done talking, read the passage one more time.

Contemplatio: Open your heart to conversation with God. What does God want to give you? Or what might he be communicating to you? Don't talk; just be open to receive.

QUESTIONS FOR JOURNALING

1. When I think of the animals as created by God with purpose and intention, how do I see them differently?
2. How do I see myself differently, surrounded by God's creatures?
3. My strongest thought, feeling, or desire during prayer was …
4. I sensed God communicating to me …

_____

_____

_____

_____

_____

_____

_____

_____

_____

_____

_____

_____

_____

_____

_____

_____

Close with a brief conversation giving thanks to God for your prayer experience. You may be tempted to skip this, as you've already talked to God. But keep in mind that the goal of prayer is not to have nice notes in a journal, but to have a deeper encounter with the God who loves you. So after praying, reflecting, and journaling, have one more little chat with God. Think of it like talking to a friend as you walk them out to their car after a nice visit. Thanks, God! Then pray one Our Father.

December 3 — Thursday
Thursday of the First Week of Advent

SAINT FRANCIS XAVIER

A native of Spain, Francis Xavier met Saint Ignatius of Loyola while studying at the University of Paris. He became one of the first seven members of the Society of Jesus (the Jesuits). He was sent to preach the Gospel in the Orient. His travels took him to India and Japan, and in ten years of missionary work, he brought over thirty thousand souls to the light of Christ. He died on the doorstep of China. He is a patron saint of missions.

Preparation: Come, Holy Spirit, enlighten the eyes of my heart.

Lectio: Read the passage slowly and prayerfully.

GENESIS 1:26–28

Then God said: Let us make human beings in our image, after our likeness. Let them have dominion over the fish of the sea, the birds of the air, the tame animals, all the wild animals, and all the creatures that crawl on the earth.

God created mankind in his image;
in the image of God he created them;
male and female he created them.

God blessed them and God said to them: Be fertile and multiply; fill the earth and subdue it. Have dominion over the fish of the sea, the birds of the air, and all the living things that crawl on the earth.

Meditatio: God pauses to think before he creates the next thing. Human beings are the crown of creation. In their intellect and free will, they are images of God. If you want to know what God looks like, look in the mirror. Sit back and think: I am an image of God.

And so is every person on this earth. Even those who know nothing of God are made in his image. Our sin can erase the likeness of God but not the image of God. Yet we are meant to be both image and likeness. Read the passage again slowly.

Oratio: What is this prayer time stirring up inside you? Chew on your thoughts a little bit, then talk to God. Tell him what you are thinking and feeling. Share your heart with the One who made it. When you are done talking, read the passage one more time.

Contemplatio: Open your heart to conversation with God. What does God want to give you or say to you? Don't try too hard to "get it." Just be open to receive.

QUESTIONS FOR JOURNALING

1. I am surrounded by God's beautiful creatures, but I too am a beautiful creation. How does it feel to be a creation of the Creator?
2. How does it change my view of myself to think of God as the artist and myself as his handiwork, a unique and unrepeatable masterpiece?
3. I sensed God wanted me to know …
4. I struggled with …
5. I ended prayer wanting …

Close with a brief conversation giving thanks to God for your prayer experience. Then pray an Our Father.

December 4 — Friday
Friday of the First Week of Advent

Preparation: Come, Holy Spirit, enlighten the eyes of my heart.

Lectio: God not only created the world, but he also governs it. The sun shines on all creation, sees all things, and provides warmth and light to all things. In a similar way, God looks down from the heavens and sees and hears everything. He governs all things, providing commands that guide us wisely.

Read the passage slowly and prayerfully.

PSALM 19:2–12

The heavens declare the glory of God;
  the firmament proclaims the works of his hands.
Day unto day pours forth speech;
  night unto night whispers knowledge.
There is no speech, no words;
  their voice is not heard;
A report goes forth through all the earth,
  their messages, to the ends of the world.
He has pitched in them a tent for the sun;
  it comes forth like a bridegroom from his canopy,
  and like a hero joyfully runs its course.
From one end of the heavens it comes forth;
  its course runs through to the other;
  nothing escapes its heat.

The law of the LORD is perfect,
  refreshing the soul.
The decree of the LORD is trustworthy,
  giving wisdom to the simple.
The precepts of the LORD are right,

> *rejoicing the heart.*
> *The command of the LORD is clear,*
> *enlightening the eye.*
> *The fear of the LORD is pure,*
> *enduring forever.*
> *The statutes of the LORD are true,*
> *all of them just;*
> *More desirable than gold,*
> *than a hoard of purest gold,*
> *Sweeter also than honey*
> *or drippings from the comb.*
> *By them your servant is warned;*
> *obeying them brings much reward.*

Meditatio: God hears and sees all things, even a whisper. Does that realization give me comfort or make me uncomfortable? Do I see God's words as creative and life-giving? Do I meditate on God's laws and draw wisdom and sustenance from them? Or do I see the law of God as something oppressive and burdensome?

God is not only active in the world but active in our lives. When have you noticed God's presence and action guiding and governing your life? Read the passage again slowly.

Oratio: God hears all things. What do you want to say to him? Speak from your heart. When you are done speaking, read the passage one more time.

Contemplatio: Open your heart to receive what God wants to say to you. Maybe it is a thought, a word, or a sense of peace. Maybe you just feel more grateful. Spend a moment receiving.

QUESTIONS FOR JOURNALING
1. I obeyed God and experienced much reward when …
2. My strongest thought, feeling, or desire during prayer was …
3. I struggle with …

4. I sensed God communicating to me …
5. I ended prayer wanting …

Close with a brief conversation giving thanks to God for your prayer experience. Then pray an Our Father.

December 5 — Saturday
Saturday of the First Week of Advent

REVIEW

Preparation: Come, Holy Spirit, enlighten the eyes of my heart.

Let's take some time to savor the Lord's presence. Flip through your past week's journal entries. Notice what emerged in the conversations. Here are some questions to help you:

1. Where did I notice the presence and action of God?
2. What was he doing, saying, or giving me?
3. How did I respond to what God was doing?
4. I really struggled with …
5. Prayer really seemed to click when …
6. I'm grateful for …

Is there one clear image of God's loving presence that emerged from your prayer during this first week?

Savor that image of God's loving presence. Rest there for a minute or two. Then close with an Our Father.

Week Two

Relational Prayer (ARRR)

I hope you enjoyed *lectio divina*. Week two will be devoted to a new form of prayer called Relational Prayer or "A-R-R-R." This prayer form has four steps:

Acknowledge what is going on inside you: your thoughts, feelings, and desires.

Relate or share with the Lord what is going on inside you.

Receive what God wants to give you.

Respond to what the Lord just gave you.

This form of prayer focuses less on the text and more on what is going on inside you. As you read the text, what are you thinking about? What are you feeling? Look at yourself, and take your pulse, as it were, emotionally speaking. Use your thoughts and emotions as a conversation starter.

"Relate" is the step at which you share with the Lord the thoughts, feelings, and desires that you have noticed. The relating shifts your attention from yourself to the Lord. I "give it all to Jesus" and look at him, knowing that he is looking at me. I open my heart to receive whatever he wants to give me.

This prayer form can be a little more challenging than *lectio divina*. Be patient with it, and see what happens.

Grace of the Week: We are surrounded by God's creation. But we are also creatures, created by God the Father and made for a relationship with him. This week we will explore our fall from a relationship with God and into the deep darkness of sin and death. Pray for the grace to understand the pain of separation from God and thereby experience a deeper longing for him.

December 6 — Sunday
Second Sunday of Advent

SAINT NICHOLAS, BISHOP

Saint Nicholas was the bishop of Myra, in modern-day Turkey. He died on this day around A.D. 350. He is one of the most popular Christian saints, though very little is known about him. He is a patron of mariners, merchants, bakers, travelers, and children. There are many legends associated with him, one of which is that he brings little gifts to children on his feast day.

Preparation: Come, Holy Spirit, enlighten the eyes of my heart.

Flip back to that one image of God's loving presence that emerged in your prayer on Saturday. Spend about a minute resting there and living in that moment.

Acknowledge: As you read the following passage, notice what stirs inside you: thoughts, feelings, desires.

2 PETER 3:8–14

But do not ignore this one fact, beloved, that with the Lord one day is like a thousand years and a thousand years like one day. The Lord does not delay his promise, as some regard "delay," but he is patient with you, not wishing that any should perish but that all should come to repentance. But the day of the Lord will come like a thief, and then the heavens will pass away with a mighty roar and the elements will be dissolved by fire, and the earth and everything done on it will be found out.

Since everything is to be dissolved in this way, what sort of persons ought [you] to be, conducting yourselves in holiness and devotion, waiting for and hastening the coming of the day of God, because of which the heavens will be dissolved in flames and the elements melted by *fire. But according to his promise we await new heavens and a new earth in which righteousness dwells.*

Therefore, beloved, since you await these things, be eager to be found without spot or blemish before him, at peace.

Relate: Read the passage a second time. Notice the strongest thought, feeling, or desire.

God is with you right here and right now. Turn your mind to him. Speak to him in your heart. Share with him whatever thought, feeling, or desire was stirred up by the passage above.

I find "relating" to be the most difficult step of this form of prayer. The key here is to shift your attention to God. Think of it this way: As you're reading through this passage, you become aware of a good friend leaning over your shoulder, looking at it with you. You invite the friend to sit down. Tell him what you noticed in the passage. Then look at him and ask what he noticed. Your attention shifts from you, the passage, and your thoughts to Our Lord.

Receive: What is in God's heart for you? How does God respond to what you have related to him? Read the passage a third time.

Respond: Receive what God has to give you, then answer him. It may be just a simple "Thank you," or it may move to deeper conversation: whatever you and God have in mind.

QUESTIONS FOR JOURNALING

1. What jumped out at me when I first read the passage was …
2. My strongest thought, feeling, or desire during prayer was …
3. I sensed God communicating to me …
4. I found the whole experience of prayer today to be …
5. I ended prayer wanting …

_____

_____

_____

_____

_____

_____

_____

_____

_____

_____

_____

_____

_____

_____

_____

_____

_____

_____

Close with a brief conversation giving thanks to God for your prayer experience. Then pray an Our Father.

December 7 — Monday
Monday of the Second Week of Advent

Preparation: Come, Holy Spirit, enlighten the eyes of my heart.

Go back to that image of God's loving presence that emerged in your prayer on Saturday. Spend about a minute resting there and living in the moment.

Acknowledge: The passage here is like the previous story of creation but different. This time there is a command from God and a warning that comes with it. Notice what the reading stirs inside you: thoughts, feelings, desires.

GENESIS 2:7–9, 16–17

Then the LORD God formed the man out of the dust of the ground and blew into his nostrils the breath of life, and the man became a living being.

The LORD God planted a garden in Eden, in the east, and placed there the man whom he had formed. Out of the ground the LORD God made grow every tree that was delightful to look at and good for food, with the tree of life in the middle of the garden and the tree of the knowledge of good and evil. ...

The LORD God gave the man this order: You are free to eat from any of the trees of the garden except the tree of knowledge of good and evil. From that tree you shall not eat; when you eat from it you shall die.

Relate: Read the passage a second time. Notice the strongest thought, feeling, or desire.

God is with you right here and right now. Turn your mind to God. Speak to him in your heart as you might talk to a good friend. Share with him the thoughts, feelings, or desires that were stirred up in the passage above.

Receive: Your attention moves from your thoughts to the God who created you and has revealed his love for you. What is in God's heart for you? How does God respond to what you have related to him? If you find yourself stuck, don't try too hard to "figure out" what God might be saying. Maybe all he wants to give you is a feeling of peace or a new awareness. Whatever it is, receive it. Read the passage a third time.

Respond: Receive what God has to give you, then answer him. It may be a simple "Thank you." Or it may be moving to deeper conversation. It's like spending time with a good friend.

QUESTIONS FOR JOURNALING
1. What jumped out at me when I first read the passage was ...
2. My strongest thought, feeling, or desire during prayer was ...
3. I sensed God communicating to me ...
4. I found the whole experience of prayer today to be ...
5. I ended prayer wanting ...

Close with a brief conversation giving thanks to God for your prayer experience. Then pray an Our Father.

December 8 — Tuesday
Solemnity of the Immaculate Conception

The Christian Church has long believed that the Blessed Virgin Mary was preserved free from all sin, starting at the very moment of her conception. Christians have celebrated this feast for over twelve hundred years, but the Immaculate Conception was only declared a dogma in 1854, by Pope Blessed Pius IX. Four years later, Our Lady appeared to Saint Bernadette at Lourdes, France, and told her, "I am the Immaculate Conception."

Today's feast is a holy day of obligation for Catholics, and the Gloria is sung at Mass.

Preparation: Come, Holy Spirit, enlighten the eyes of my heart.

Call to mind that image of God's loving presence that emerged in your prayer last week. Spend about a minute resting in God's unconditional love for you.

Acknowledge: Read the passage below. As you read, notice what it stirs inside you: thoughts, feelings desires. How does it feel for Adam to be caught red-handed, feeling naked and afraid of God? When have you felt guilty, ashamed, naked? Are there feelings, or perhaps memories of an experience, that reading this passage stirs up? If nothing personal comes to mind, imagine how Adam and Eve would have felt.

GENESIS 3:9–15, 20

The LORD God then called to the man and asked him: Where are you? He answered, "I heard you in the garden; but I was afraid, because I was naked, so I hid." Then God asked: Who told you that you were naked? Have you eaten from the tree of which I had forbidden you to eat? The man replied, "The woman whom you put here with me — she gave me fruit from the tree, so I ate it." The LORD God then asked the woman: What is this you have done? The woman answered, "The snake tricked me, so I ate it."

*Then the L*ORD *God said to the snake:*
Because you have done this,
cursed are you
among all the animals, tame or wild;
On your belly you shall crawl,
and dust you shall eat
all the days of your life.
I will put enmity between you and the woman,
and between your offspring and hers;
They will strike at your head,
while you strike at their heel. ...

The man gave his wife the name "Eve," because she was the mother of all the living.

Relate: Read the passage a second time. Notice your strongest thought, feeling, or desire.

God is with you right here and right now. There is no need to be afraid of him or hide from him. Turn your heart to God. Speak to him in your heart. Share with him what this passage stirred up in you. Sometimes the biggest feeling might be that you don't want to share your feelings with God. If that is the case, can you tell God that?

Receive: Read the passage a third time. This time receive whatever is in God's heart for you: his thoughts, feelings, desires. If you find yourself struggling, know that you don't have to try so hard. Just be open to receive. Many times God gives something simple like a feeling of peace, a sense of his presence, or a sense that he understands what we are going through.

Respond: Receive what God has to give you, then answer him again. It may be just a simple "Thank you, or you may have more to talk about. Enjoy the presence of God for a minute or two before moving on.

QUESTIONS FOR JOURNALING

1. My strongest thought, feeling, or desire during prayer was …
2. I sensed God communicating to me …
3. I ended prayer wanting …

Close with a brief conversation giving thanks to God for your prayer experience. Then pray an Our Father.

December 9 — Wednesday
Wednesday of the Second Week of Advent

Preparation: Come, Holy Spirit, enlighten the eyes of my heart.

Call to mind an image of God's loving presence that has emerged in your prayer. Spend about a minute resting in God's merciful love for you.

Acknowledge: Adam and Eve are sentenced to hard labor — for her the labor of bearing children, for him the labor of tilling the earth. Because of Adam and Eve, men and women continue to toil and labor. Raising children, buying Christmas gifts, figuring out a way to pay for them all: Feel the heaviness of the sentence that will rest on human beings of all generations. When do you feel yourself toiling under a heavy burden?

Remember that God is more than a judge. He is a Father deeply grieved by his children's sinfulness. He starts to unfold a plan to remedy their sinfulness. Christians have long believed that Jesus' death forgave even Adam and Eve and that God took them to heaven in the end.

Read the passage, noting what stirs inside you: thoughts, feelings, desires.

GENESIS 3:16–19

To the woman he said:
I will intensify your toil in childbearing;
in pain you shall bring forth children.
Yet your urge shall be for your husband,
and he shall rule over you.

To the man he said: Because you listened to your wife and ate from the tree about which I commanded you, You shall not eat from it,
Cursed is the ground because of you!
In toil you shall eat its yield
all the days of your life.

Thorns and thistles it shall bear for you,
*   and you shall eat the grass of the field.*
By the sweat of your brow
*   you shall eat bread,*
Until you return to the ground,
*   from which you were taken;*
For you are dust,
*   and to dust you shall return.*

Relate: Read the passage a second time, aware that God is with you here and now. Turn your heart to him. Speak to him there. Share with him the burdens that you carry.

Receive: Open your heart to receive whatever is in God's heart for you: his thoughts, feelings, or desires. He loves you and is with you in the midst of your burdens. Be open to receive, without fear or expectation. Read the passage a third time.

Respond: Receive what God has for you, then answer him. It may be just a simple "Thank you," or it may move to deeper conversation. Be with the Lord for a minute or two before moving on.

QUESTIONS FOR JOURNALING
1. My strongest thought, feeling, or desire was …
2. I feel burdened when …
3. I see the love of God in a new way …
4. I sensed God communicating to me …
5. A new insight or understanding I received was …

Close with a brief conversation giving thanks to God for your prayer experience. Then pray an Our Father.

December 10 — Thursday
Thursday of the Second Week of Advent

Preparation: Come, Holy Spirit, enlighten the eyes of my heart.

Call to mind an image of God's loving presence, and spend the first minute of your prayer resting in the free, unearned gift of loving and being loved.

Acknowledge: As you read the passage, notice what stirs inside you: thoughts, feelings, desires. Feel the injustice of a people who run from the true God, a people who thank other gods for blessings the Lord has given.

How often do you thank the government, your paycheck, or your own hard work and ingenuity for things that are actually gifts from your loving Father? How have you turned the season of Advent from a preparation for Christ into an excuse for commercialism and excess?

HOSEA 11:1-7

When Israel was a child I loved him,
out of Egypt I called my son.
The more I called them,
the farther they went from me,
Sacrificing to the Baals
and burning incense to idols.
Yet it was I who taught Ephraim to walk,
who took them in my arms;
but they did not know that I cared for them.
I drew them with human cords,
with bands of love;
I fostered them like those
who raise an infant to their cheeks;
I bent down to feed them.

He shall return to the land of Egypt,

> *Assyria shall be his king,*
> *because they have refused to repent.*
> *The sword shall rage in his cities:*
> *it shall destroy his diviners,*
> *and devour them because of their schemings.*
> *My people have their mind set on apostasy;*
> *though they call on God in unison,*
> *he shall not raise them up.*

Relate: Read the passage a second time, and notice your strongest thought, feeling, or desire. Turn your heart to God, and speak to him. Share with him what this passage stirred up in you.

Now let God look at you with love. How does he respond to you?

Receive: Open your heart to receive whatever is in God's heart for you: his thoughts, feelings, desires. Has God been drawing you with "bands of love" during your Advent journey? How has God been caring for you and blessing you, even when you didn't deserve it? Read the passage a third time.

Respond: Receive what God has for you, and answer him, perhaps just letting him know that you have heard him. Or perhaps your response is to spend time with the One who loves you. Perhaps he is inviting you to some kind of action. Be with the Lord for a minute or two before moving on.

QUESTIONS FOR JOURNALING

1. A new insight or understanding I received was …
2. I felt convicted that …
3. I sensed God communicating to me …
4. I see the love of God present …
5. I feel the Spirit of God moving me to a new way of acting, responding, or thinking …

Close with a brief conversation giving thanks to God for your prayer experience. Then pray an Our Father.

December 11 — Friday
Friday of the Second Week of Advent

Preparation: Come, Holy Spirit, enlighten the eyes of my heart.

Call to mind God's loving presence, and spend the first minute of your prayer resting in the free, unearned gift of loving and being loved.

Acknowledge: God is not content to let us run forever. He will never tire of searching for his lost sheep. God has an answer to our sinfulness, to the anguish of Eve and the sweat of Adam. His answer is to send a child, who will grow up to be our Savior.

The people cannot remove their own yoke; it is God who will break the yoke of the taskmaster. He will set his people free, not only from Egyptians but from sin and death itself. How good God is!

As you read this passage, notice what stirs inside you: thoughts, feelings, desires.

ISAIAH 9:1-6

The people who walked in darkness
      have seen a great light;
Upon those who lived in a land of gloom
      a light has shone.
You have brought them abundant joy
      and great rejoicing;
They rejoice before you as people rejoice at harvest,
      as they exult when dividing the spoils.
For the yoke that burdened them,
      the pole on their shoulder,
The rod of their taskmaster,
      you have smashed, as on the day of Midian.
For every boot that tramped in battle,
      every cloak rolled in blood,
      will be burned as fuel for fire.

For a child is born to us, a son is given to us;
upon his shoulder dominion rests.
They name him Wonder-Counselor, God-Hero,
Father-Forever, Prince of Peace.
His dominion is vast
and forever peaceful,
Upon David's throne, and over his kingdom,
which he confirms and sustains
By judgment and justice,
both now and forever.
The zeal of the LORD of hosts will do this!

Relate: Read the passage a second time. Turn your heart to God, and speak to him. Share with him what this passage stirred up in you. He knows your sins, your failures, your fears, and the ways you have rejected his love. But he loves you anyway! Now let him look at you with love. How does he respond?

Receive: Turn from your feelings to the presence of God, and receive whatever is in God's heart for you: his thoughts, feelings, desires. Read the passage a third time.

Respond: Receive what God has for you, then respond to him. Rest with the Lord for a minute or two before moving on.

QUESTIONS FOR JOURNALING
1. A new insight or understanding I received was …
2. I sensed God communicating to me …
3. I have a hard time accepting the fact that …
4. I am excited about …
5. I feel the Spirit of God moving me to a new way of acting, responding, or thinking …

Close with a brief conversation, giving thanks to God for your prayer experience. Then pray an Our Father.

December 12 — Saturday
Feast of Our Lady of Guadalupe

In 1531, the Blessed Virgin Mary appeared to an Aztec Indian convert named Juan Diego. He was to tell the bishop to build a church on that location. As proof of her message, Mary provided a miraculous image of herself painted on his cloak. Millions travel every year to the shrine near Mexico City where Saint Juan Diego's cloak still hangs with the miraculous image plainly visible.

Our Lady of Guadalupe is the patroness of the Americas. She reminds us that God has made a far more precious image in each of us. How has the Master Artist been working in your life this past week?

REVIEW
Preparation: Come, Holy Spirit, enlighten the eyes of my heart.

Flip through your past week's journal entries. As you do, notice what emerged in the conversations. Here are some questions to help you:

1. Where did I notice God, and what was he doing or saying?
2. How did I respond to what God was doing?
3. I really struggled with …
4. Prayer really seemed to click when …
5. I'm grateful for …
6. Now, at the end of this Second Week of Advent, what new meaning is Christmas taking on for you?

7. What image of God's loving presence sticks with you most strongly?

Conclude by conversing with God about your week. Acknowledge what you have been experiencing. Relate it to him. Receive what he wants to give you. Respond to him. Then savor that image of God's loving presence, and rest there for a minute or two. Close with an Our Father.

Week Three

Imaginative Prayer

You may have found yourself struggling a little more in Week Two compared to Week One. If so, don't be discouraged. Oftentimes the first few days of a pilgrimage can be great fun. But then we can encounter resistance. We can be discouraged by our lack of progress, by unmet expectations, or by a seeming fruitlessness in prayer. We might start making excuses not to pray.

Resistance is part of the journey and even a sign of progress. If you encounter resistance, it is probably a sign that you are on the right road. Keep walking!

The other reason you may have struggled is that ARRR isn't a great way to pray with Scripture; rather it forms a building block for our next form of prayer: imaginative prayer.

Many people are skeptical of imaginative prayer. They wonder if they are inventing things and if God is really speaking to them through their prayer. Yet your imagination was created by God as a faculty of the intellect. It is a powerful tool and can be used to make Scripture come alive.

Remember that prayer is really about spending time with the God who loves us. It's not about filling pages of a journal with amazing insights or experiences. If you are open to an encounter, then God will come and meet you. The imagination is only a conversation starter. Like *meditatio* and the Relating step of ARRR, it can open you up to an encounter with God.

Grace of the Week: God has a plan to restore creation and undo the effects of sin. We will spend the first few days of this week looking at the plans and promises God has made to find his lost sheep. Pray for the grace of a deepening desire for God and a willingness to wait patiently until his plans for you unfold in their fullness.

December 13 — Sunday
Third Sunday of Advent

Preparation: Come, Holy Spirit, enlighten the eyes of my heart.

Remind your heart of God's loving presence, and spend the first minute of your prayer resting in the free, unearned gift of loving and being loved.

Set the Scene: As you read the passage, set the scene in your mind. John was clothed in camel's hair and ate locusts and wild honey. He was out in the wilderness preaching repentance. Crowds gathered along the bank of the Jordan River to be baptized by him.

Spend a few minutes building this scene in your imagination. What does the wilderness look like, feel like, smell like?

JOHN 1:6–8, 19–28

A man named John was sent from God. He came for testimony, to testify to the light, so that all might believe through him. He was not the light, but came to testify to the light. ...

And this is the testimony of John. When the Jews from Jerusalem sent priests and Levites [to him] to ask him, "Who are you?" he admitted and did not deny it, but admitted, "I am not the Messiah." So they asked him, "What are you then? Are you Elijah?" And he said, "I am not." "Are you the Prophet?" He answered, "No." So they said to him, "Who are you, so we can give an answer to those who sent us? What do you have to say for yourself?" He said:

"I am 'the voice of one crying out in the desert,
"Make straight the way of the Lord,"'

as Isaiah the prophet said." Some Pharisees were also sent. They asked him, "Why then do you baptize if you are *not the Messiah or Elijah or the Prophet?" John answered them, "I baptize with water; but there is one among you whom you do not recognize, the one who is coming after me, whose sandal strap I am not worthy to untie." This happened in Bethany across the Jordan, where John was baptizing.*

Action! Read the passage a second time. See the priests, Levites, and Pharisees approaching to question John. Hear his confident response: The Messiah is already among us.

Place yourself in the scene. Feel the sun beating down on you, and smell the Jordan River. Where are you most comfortable: with the crowds lining up for baptism? among the priests and Pharisees? sitting at a comfortable distance, watching it all unfold but trying not to get involved?

Acknowledge: Now we will use your ARRR skills from last week. Read the passage a third time. Notice your strongest thought, feeling, or desire.

Relate: John announces that the long-awaited Messiah is coming to be with you. How does that make you feel? Share with Jesus your expectations. Let him look at you with love. How does he respond?

Receive: Receive whatever is in God's heart for you: his thoughts, feelings, desires.

Respond: Now answer him. Be with the Lord for a minute or two before moving on.

QUESTIONS FOR JOURNALING
1. While imagining the scene, what stood out to me was …
2. When the Pharisees entered the scene, I felt …
3. I sensed God communicating to me …
4. Jesus is with me when …
5. Jesus is calling me to …

_____

_____

_____

_____

_____

_____

_____

_____

_____

_____

_____

_____

_____

_____

_____

_____

Close with a brief conversation, giving thanks to God for your prayer experience. Then pray an Our Father.

December 14 — Monday
Monday of the Third Week of Advent

Preparation: Come, Holy Spirit, enlighten the eyes of my heart.

Remind your heart of God's loving presence, and spend the first minute of your prayer resting in the free, unearned gift of loving and being loved.

Set the Scene: As you read the passage, set the scene in your mind. The King is coming; a highway must be prepared for him. This King is also a shepherd, who comes to feed the sheep, gather them, and care for them.

ISAIAH 40:1-3, 9B-11

Comfort, give comfort to my people,
*　　says your God.*
Speak to the heart of Jerusalem, and proclaim to her
*　　　　that her service has ended,*
*　　　　that her guilt is expiated,*
That she has received from the hand of the Lord
*　　double for all her sins.*

*　　A voice proclaims:*
In the wilderness prepare the way of the Lord!
*　　Make straight in the wasteland a highway for our God! ...*

Cry out, do not fear!
*　　Say to the cities of Judah:*
*　　　　Here is your God!*
Here comes with power
*　　the* Lord God,
*　　who rules by his strong arm;*
Here is his reward with him,

> *his recompense before him.*
> *Like a shepherd he feeds his flock;*
> *in his arms he gathers the lambs,*
> *Carrying them in his bosom,*
> *leading the ewes with care.*

Action! Read the passage a second time, placing yourself in the scene. You probably have no choice but to be a sheep! Are you running toward the shepherd, excited? Or are you running away from him in fear? Will you let him feed, carry, and lead you?

Acknowledge: Read the passage a third time. How does it feel to be a sheep? Notice your strongest thought, feeling, or desire.

Relate: Speak to the Shepherd about what is on your heart. Let him look at you with love. How does he respond?

Receive: Receive whatever is in God's heart for you — his thoughts, feelings, desires.

Respond: Now answer him. Be with the Lord for a minute or two before moving on.

QUESTIONS FOR JOURNALING
1. My strongest thought, feeling, or desire was …
2. One fear that I noticed was …
3. God was responding to me by …
4. I felt the love of God most strongly when …
5. The Shepherd is inviting me to …

Close with a brief conversation giving thanks to God for your prayer experience. Then pray an Our Father.

December 15 — Tuesday
Tuesday of the Third Week of Advent

Preparation: Come, Holy Spirit, enlighten the eyes of my heart.

Remind your heart of God's loving presence, and spend the first minute of your prayer resting in the free, unearned gift of loving and being loved.

Set the Scene: As you read the passage, picture the scattered sheep on the hillsides, far from their own country.

EZEKIEL 34:11–15

For thus says the Lord GOD: Look! I myself will search for my sheep and examine them. As a shepherd examines his flock while he himself is among his scattered sheep, so will I examine my sheep. I will deliver them from every place where they were scattered on the day of dark clouds. I will lead them out from among the peoples and gather them from the lands; I will bring them back to their own country and pasture them upon the mountains of Israel, in the ravines and every inhabited place in the land. In good pastures I will pasture them; on the mountain heights of Israel will be their grazing land. There they will lie down on good grazing ground; in rich pastures they will be pastured on the mountains of Israel. I myself will pasture my sheep; I myself will give them rest — oracle of the Lord GOD.

Action! Read the passage a second time, placing yourself in the scene. What does it feel like to be scattered when it is cloudy and dark? What does it feel like to lie down on good grazing ground? In what ways do you desire rest this Advent season?

Acknowledge: Read the passage a third time. Notice your strongest thought, feeling, or desire.

Relate: Speak to the Shepherd about what is on your heart. Let him look at you with love. How does he respond?

Receive: Receive whatever is in God's heart for you — his thoughts, feelings, desires.

Respond: Now answer him. Be with the Lord for a minute or two before moving on.

QUESTIONS FOR JOURNALING
1. My heart desires more than anything …
2. My greatest fear or struggle seems to be …
3. I sensed God communicating to me …
4. Today I sensed the Shepherd inviting me to …

_____

_____

_____

_____

_____

_____

_____

_____

_____

_____

_____

_____

_____

_____

_____

_____

_____

Close with a brief conversation giving thanks to God for your prayer experience. Then pray an Our Father.

December 16 — Wednesday

Wednesday of the Third Week of Advent

Preparation: Come, Holy Spirit, enlighten the eyes of my heart.

Remind your heart of God's loving presence, and spend the first minute of your prayer resting in the free, unearned gift of loving and being loved.

Set the Scene: Read the passage. You don't have to pretend to be a sheep. Think of green pastures and still waters, an afternoon nap in a field.

PSALM 23

The LORD is my shepherd;
    there is nothing I lack.
In green pastures he makes me lie down;
    to still waters he leads me;
    he restores my soul.
He guides me along right paths
    for the sake of his name.
Even though I walk through the valley of the shadow of death,
    I will fear no evil, for you are with me;
    your rod and your staff comfort me.
You set a table before me
    in front of my enemies;
You anoint my head with oil;
    my cup overflows.
Indeed, goodness and mercy will pursue me
    all the days of my life;
I will dwell in the house of the LORD
    for endless days.

Action! Read the passage a second time.

Now you are walking the right paths with the Shepherd. His presence keeps the enemies away, even when it is cloudy and dark. You follow this path to the house of the Lord, where a banquet has been prepared for you. Here you find true rest for endless days.

Acknowledge: Read the passage a third time. Notice what stirs inside you. What is your strongest thought, feeling, or desire?

Relate: Speak to the Shepherd about what is on your heart. Let him look at you with love. How does he respond?

Receive: Receive whatever is in God's heart for you — his thoughts, feelings, desires.

Respond: Now answer him. Be with the Lord for a minute or two before moving on.

QUESTIONS FOR JOURNALING
1. I found strength and comfort when …
2. True peace for me would look like …
3. I sensed God communicating to me …
4. God wants to give me …

Close with a brief conversation giving thanks to God for your prayer experience. Then pray an Our Father.

December 17 — Thursday
Countdown to Christmas: Nine

O Wisdom of our God Most High,
guiding creation with power and love:
come to teach us the path of knowledge!

Each day from December 17 to December 23 is assigned a special "O Antiphon," a poetic invocation that names who the coming Messiah is and what he will do, drawing on imagery from Old Testament prophecies. At this time, the Advent season switches gears. The lectionary gives us readings from the Gospel passages that immediately precede the birth of Jesus. We will pray with these readings, using imaginative prayer, *lectio divina*, and ARRR.

Preparation: Come, Holy Spirit, enlighten the eyes of my heart.

Be present to the God who is always present to you. Call to mind his loving care for you, and spend the first minute of your prayer resting in the free, unearned gift of loving and being loved.

Lectio: Read the passage slowly and prayerfully. Underline the names you recognize.

MATTHEW 1:1-17

The book of the genealogy of Jesus Christ, the son of David, the son of Abraham.

Abraham became the father of Isaac, Isaac the father of Jacob, Jacob the father of Judah and his brothers. Judah became the father of Perez and Zerah, whose mother was Tamar. Perez became the father of Hezron, Hezron the father of Ram, Ram the father of Amminad-

ab. Amminadab became the father of Nahshon, Nahshon the father of Salmon, Salmon the father of Boaz, whose mother was Rahab. Boaz became the father of Obed, whose mother was Ruth. Obed became the father of Jesse, Jesse the father of David the king.

David became the father of Solomon, whose mother had been the wife of Uriah. Solomon became the father of Rehoboam, Rehoboam the father of Abijah, Abijah the father of Asaph. Asaph became the father of Jehoshaphat, Jehoshaphat the father of Joram, Joram the father of Uzziah. Uzziah became the father of Jotham, Jotham the father of Ahaz, Ahaz the father of Hezekiah. Hezekiah became the father of Manasseh, Manasseh the father of Amos, Amos the father of Josiah. Josiah became the father of Jechoniah and his brothers at the time of the Babylonian exile.

After the Babylonian exile, Jechoniah became the father of Shealtiel, Shealtiel the father of Zerubbabel, Zerubbabel the father of Abiud. Abiud became the father of Eliakim, Eliakim the father of Azor, Azor the father of Zadok. Zadok became the father of Achim, Achim the father of Eliud, Eliud the father of Eleazar. Eleazar became the father of Matthan, Matthan the father of Jacob, Jacob the father of Joseph, the husband of Mary. Of her was born Jesus who is called the Christ.

Thus the total number of generations from Abraham to David is fourteen generations; from David to the Babylonian exile, fourteen generations; from the Babylonian exile to the Christ, fourteen generations. (Lectionary)

Meditatio: We might roll our eyes at these passages because of all the unrecognized and unpronounceable names. But these were real people who were born, lived their life, had children, and died. Their bones are buried somewhere. Some of them are famous saints, and others are rather infamous. Yet God used each of them to bring about the birth of his Son. All along, he was "guiding creation with power and love," as today's

O Antiphon says.

What does your bloodline look like? How might God be using you, and other ordinary people, in extraordinary ways? Reflect for a few minutes, then read the passage again slowly.

Oratio: Speak to God what is on your heart and mind. Then read the passage one more time.

Contemplatio: Open your heart to receive what God wants to give you. Maybe it is a thought, a word, or a sense of peace. Maybe you also will have a bit of conversation.

God is with you in this ordinary moment. Rest in and savor his love for you.

QUESTIONS FOR JOURNALING

1. I see God's hand in my own personal history when …
2. Because of my family or past, I struggle with …
3. I sensed God communicating to me …
4. I ended prayer wanting …

Close with a brief conversation to thank God for your prayer experience. Then pray an Our Father.

December 18 — Friday
Countdown to Christmas: Eight

O Leader of the House of Israel,
giver of the Law to Moses on Sinai:
come to rescue us with your mighty power!

Preparation: Come, Holy Spirit, enlighten the eyes of my heart.

Be present to the God who is always present to you. Call to mind his loving care for you, and spend the first minute of your prayer resting in the free, unearned gift of loving and being loved.

Set the Scene: As you read the passage, set the scene in your mind. Mary went to visit her cousin Elizabeth and was absent for three months (see Lk 1:56). On her return, she would have been visibly pregnant. Picture where Saint Joseph might have been when he learned this. What were his thoughts, feelings, and desires?

MATTHEW 1:18-25

Now this is how the birth of Jesus Christ came about. When his mother Mary was betrothed to Joseph, but before they lived together, she was found with child through the Holy Spirit. Joseph her husband, since he was a righteous man, yet unwilling to expose her to shame, decided to divorce her quietly. Such was his intention when, behold, the angel of the Lord appeared to him in a dream and said, "Joseph, son of David, do not be afraid to take Mary your wife into your home. For it is through the Holy Spirit that this child has been conceived in her. She will bear a son and you are to name him Jesus, because he will save his people from their sins." All this took place to fulfill what the Lord had said through the prophet:

> *Behold, the virgin shall be with child and bear a son,*
> *and they shall name him Emmanuel,*

which means "God is with us." When Joseph awoke, he did as the angel of the Lord had commanded him and took his wife into his home. He had no relations with her until she bore a son, and he named him Jesus. (Lectionary)

Action! God gave the law that ultimately put Joseph in this predicament. Yet God was also there to show him the way forward. Read the passage a second time. What does Joseph experience through his dream?

What difference does it make that "God is with us"? Has God's love entered into and changed a hopeless situation for you?

Acknowledge: Read the passage a third time. Notice your strongest thought, feeling, or desire.

Relate: Speak to the Father about what is on your heart. Let him look at you with love. How does he respond?

Receive: Receive whatever is in God's heart for you — his thoughts, feelings, desires.

Respond: Now answer him. Be with the Lord for a minute or two before moving on.

QUESTIONS FOR JOURNALING
1. I found God in the midst of struggles when …
2. My greatest fear or struggle seems to be …
3. I sensed God communicating to me …
4. I feel God's love inviting me to a new way of seeing, thinking, or acting today, as in …

Close with a brief conversation with God, giving thanks for your prayer experience. Then pray an Our Father.

December 19 — Saturday
Countdown to Christmas: Seven

O Root of Jesse's stem,
sign of God's love for all his people:
come to save us without delay!

Usually we dedicate Saturday to a review of our week. However, today's Scripture passage is too important to skip. We'll do a brief review after this meditation.

Preparation: Come, Holy Spirit, enlighten the eyes of my heart.

Be present to the God who is always present to you. Call to mind his loving care for you, and spend the first minute of your prayer resting in the free, unearned gift of loving and being loved.

Set the Scene: Read the passage, setting the scene in your mind. What does the temple look like? What does the angel look like? Picture the people outside waiting for Zechariah to emerge.

LUKE 1:5–25

In the days of Herod, King of Judea, there was a priest named Zechariah of the priestly division of Abijah; his wife was from the daughters of Aaron, and her name was Elizabeth. Both were righteous in the eyes of God, observing all the commandments and ordinances of the Lord blamelessly. But they had no child, because Elizabeth was barren and both were advanced in years.

Once when he was serving as priest in his division's turn before God, according to the practice of the priestly service, he was chosen by lot to enter the sanctuary of the

Lord to burn incense. Then, when the whole assembly of the people was praying outside at the hour of the incense offering, the angel of the Lord appeared to him, standing at the right of the altar of incense. Zechariah was troubled by what he saw, and fear came upon him.

But the angel said to him, "Do not be afraid, Zechariah, because your prayer has been heard. Your wife Elizabeth will bear you a son, and you shall name him John. And you will have joy and gladness, and many will rejoice at his birth, for he will be great in the sight of the Lord. He will drink neither wine nor strong drink. He will be filled with the Holy Spirit even from his mother's womb, and he will turn many of the children of Israel to the Lord their God. He will go before him in the spirit and power of Elijah to turn the hearts of fathers toward children and the disobedient to the understanding of the righteous, to prepare a people fit for the Lord."

Then Zechariah said to the angel, "How shall I know this? For I am an old man, and my wife is advanced in years." And the angel said to him in reply, "I am Gabriel, who stand before God. I was sent to speak to you and to announce to you this good news. But now you will be speechless and unable to talk until the day these things take place, because you did not believe my words, which will be fulfilled at their proper time."

Meanwhile the people were waiting for Zechariah and were amazed that he stayed so long in the sanctuary. But when he came out, he was unable to speak to them, and they realized that he had seen a vision in the sanctuary. He was gesturing to them but remained mute.

Then, when his days of ministry were completed, he went home.

After this time his wife Elizabeth conceived, and she went into seclusion for five months, saying, "So has the Lord done for me at a time when he has seen fit to take away my disgrace before others."

Action! Today's antiphon is drawn from Isaiah 11:1–10. King David's line has long been cut off from royal power. But God will raise up a new shoot from the "stump of Jesse" (King David's father), and "his dwelling shall be glorious."

In a similar way, Zechariah and Elizabeth have long given up the dream of having a child of their own. Even though Zechariah is a priest ministering in the temple, he does not expect an angel to meet him there. Even less is he prepared for the good news the angel brings.

Read the passage a second time, and play the scene in your mind.

Acknowledge: How does Zechariah feel about all this? How does Elizabeth feel? How do you feel? What is the desire of your heart? Read the passage a third time.

Relate: Speak to the Father about the desires of your heart. Do you believe he will fulfill them? Let him look at you with love. How does he respond?

Receive: Receive whatever is in God's heart for you — his thoughts, his feelings, his desires, his Good News for you. Do you believe that God can and will do good things in your life?

Respond: Continue the conversation. Then be with the Lord for a minute or two before moving on.

QUESTIONS FOR JOURNALING

1. I felt God stirring up a desire for ...
2. I have a hard time trusting when ...
3. My greatest fear or struggle seems to be ...
4. I sensed God was with me and wanted me to know ...

Close with a brief conversation giving thanks to God for your prayer experience. Then pray an Our Father.

A Brief Review

Take a little time at the end of your prayer today and flip back through the previous week.

1. How has God been present to me in the midst of the season's busyness?
2. Is there a particular theme that is emerging on my Advent pilgrimage?
3. What helps me stay present to God throughout the day, after my prayer time is done?
4. During the final rush to Christmas, I desire most deeply ...
5. This past week, my strongest sense, image, moment, or experience of God's loving presence was ...

Acknowledge what you have been experiencing. Relate it to the Lord. Receive what he wants to give you. Respond to him. Then savor that sense, image, moment, or experience of God's loving presence, and rest there for a minute or two. Close with an Our Father.

Week Four

The King Comes!

The text below, taken from the Roman Martyrology, presents the birth of Jesus as one would announce the birth of a king or emperor. The announcement is recited or chanted on December 24, during the celebration of the Liturgy of the Hours or before the Christmas Mass during the Night.

Let us prepare our hearts to celebrate the birth of our Savior. Come, Lord Jesus, into our hearts, our families, our world!

The Twenty-fifth Day of December, when ages beyond number had run their course from the creation of the world, when God in the beginning created heaven and earth, and formed man in his own likeness;

when century upon century had passed since the Almighty set his bow in the clouds after the Great Flood, as a sign of covenant and peace;

in the twenty-first century since Abraham, our father in faith, came out of Ur of the Chaldees;

in the thirteenth century since the People of Israel were led by Moses in the Exodus from Egypt;

around the thousandth year since David was anointed King;

in the sixty-fifth week of the prophecy of Daniel;

in the one hundred and ninety-fourth Olympiad;

in the year seven hundred and fifty-two since the foundation of the City of Rome;

in the forty-second year of the reign of Ceasar Octavian Augustus, the whole world being at peace,

Jesus Christ, eternal God and Son of the eternal Father, desiring to consecrate the world by his most loving presence, was conceived by the Holy Spirit, and when nine months had passed since his conception, was born of the Virgin Mary in Bethlehem of Judah, and was made man:

The Nativity of Our Lord Jesus Christ according to the flesh.
— *Appendix 1 of the Roman Missal, Third Edition*

Grace of the Week: Let us open our hearts to our King, who humbled himself to free all men and women from sin, Satan, and death. Pray for a deeper awareness of the great mystery of Emmanuel, God with us.

December 20 — Sunday
Fourth Sunday of Advent
Countdown to Christmas: Six

O Key of David,
opening the gates of God's eternal Kingdom:
come and free the prisoners of darkness!

Preparation: Come, Holy Spirit, enlighten the eyes of my heart.

Be present to the God who is always present to you. Call to mind his loving care for you, and spend the first minute of your prayer resting in the free, unearned gift of loving and being loved.

Set the Scene: Tradition usually sets the Annunciation at Mary's home in Nazareth. Betrothal meant that Mary and Joseph had already celebrated their wedding ceremony, but the living together (and the marital relations that typically came with it) hadn't started yet.

As you read the passage, consider what time of day it might have been. Perhaps Mary paused from her chores for a little prayer time. Use your imagination to picture the scene.

LUKE 1:26–38

The angel Gabriel was sent from God to a town of Galilee called Nazareth, to a virgin betrothed to a man named Joseph, of the house of David, and the virgin's name was Mary. And coming to her, he said, "Hail, full of grace! The Lord is with you." But she was greatly troubled at what was said and pondered what sort of greeting this might be. Then the angel said to her, "Do not be afraid, Mary, for you have found favor with God. Behold, you will conceive in your womb and bear a son, and you shall name him Jesus. He will be great and will be called Son of the Most High, and the Lord God will give him the throne of David his father, and he will rule over the house of Jacob forever, and of his Kingdom there will be no end."

But Mary said to the angel, "How can this be, since I have no relations with a man?" And the angel said to her in reply, "The Holy Spirit will come upon you, and the power of the Most High will overshadow you. Therefore the child to be born will be called holy, the Son of God. And behold, Elizabeth, your relative, has also conceived a son in her old age, and this is the sixth month for her who was called barren; for nothing will be impossible for God."

Mary said, "Behold, I am the handmaid of the Lord. May it be done to me according to your word." Then the angel departed from her. (Lectionary)

Action! Today's O Antiphon takes the Key of David (Is 22:22) in two different directions: It will open the kingdom of Heaven, which was closed by Eve's sin; and it will unlock the prisoners who have been kept in darkness by that sin. But the key doesn't have the power to unlock Mary's womb; only she can do that.

Read the passage a second time, considering all creation, groaning under the sentence of sin, awaiting Mary's answer.

Acknowledge: Why is this virgin greatly troubled at the angel's words? What is in her heart at this moment? What does her "yes" feel like? Read the passage a third time.

Relate: Do you sometimes have a hard time accepting God's plans for your life? Is God waiting for you to "unlock" your heart to him? Speak to Mary about your thoughts and feelings. Together with her, turn to the Father in prayer.

Receive: Receive whatever is in God's heart for you — his thoughts, feelings, desires. He did all for you. What more does he want to give you?

Respond: Converse with the Father in your heart. Then just be with the Lord and Mary for a minute or two before moving on.

QUESTIONS FOR JOURNALING

1. My heart is troubled by ...
2. How have I responded when God's plans interrupted my plans?
3. I sensed God was with me and wanted me to know ...
4. I ended prayer wanting ...

Close with a brief conversation with God giving thanks for your prayer experience. Then pray a Hail Mary.

December 21 — Monday
Countdown to Christmas: Five

O Radiant Dawn,
splendor of eternal light, sun of justice:
come and shine on those who dwell in
darkness and in the shadow of death.

Preparation: Come, Holy Spirit, enlighten the eyes of my heart.

Be present to the God who is always present to you. Call to mind his loving care for you. Spend the first minute of your prayer resting in the free, unearned gift of loving and being loved.

Set the Scene: Read the passage. Tradition identifies the location as a town called Ein Karem, a hill town about five miles to the west of Jerusalem and about ninety miles from Nazareth. Elizabeth is six months pregnant; Mary hasn't started to show.

LUKE 1:39–45

Mary set out in those days and traveled to the hill country in haste to a town of Judah, where she entered the house of Zechariah and greeted Elizabeth. When Elizabeth heard Mary's greeting, the infant leaped in her womb, and Elizabeth, filled with the Holy Spirit, cried out in a loud voice and said, "Most blessed are you among women, and blessed is the fruit of your womb. And how does this happen to me, that the mother of my Lord should come to me? For at the moment the sound of your greeting reached my ears, the infant in my womb leaped for joy. Blessed are you who believed that what was spoken to you by the Lord would be fulfilled." (Lectionary)

Action! "Emmanuel" means "God with us" (Is 7:14). How was God with Mary on her journey to visit Elizabeth? How does Elizabeth feel in the presence of her infant Lord? Read the passage a second time, playing the scene in your mind.

Acknowledge: Christmas is a busy time for visiting and receiving visitors. Do your visitors bring the presence of Jesus to your home, or do they bring worries of being judged? How do you bring Jesus to the homes of others?

Read the passage a third time. When have you leapt for joy at God's presence?

Relate: Let your thoughts and feelings rise to the surface. Speak to God what is in your heart.

Receive: How does the Father view this scene? How does he gaze on your visits and visitors? Receive whatever is in God's heart for you—his thoughts, feelings, desires.

Respond: Converse with the Father in your heart. Then savor the presence of Jesus for a minute or two before moving on.

QUESTIONS FOR JOURNALING
1. My heart leaped for joy when …
2. I sensed God saying to me …
3. Is there a way I can "go in haste" to share with another the joy I am receiving through these Advent prayer times?
4. I ended prayer wanting …

Close with a brief conversation with God, giving thanks for your prayer experience. Then pray a Hail Mary.

December 22 — Tuesday
Countdown to Christmas: Four

O King of all nations and keystone of the Church:
come and save man, whom you formed from the dust!

Preparation: Come, Holy Spirit, enlighten the eyes of my heart.

Be present to the God who is always present to you. Call to mind his loving care for you, and spend the first minute of your prayer resting in the free, unearned gift of loving and being loved.

Lectio: This Scripture is called the Magnificat (the first word of the passage in Latin). It is a hymn of praise to God who has been faithful to his promises from Abraham until today. This could very well be a song that the saints sing in heaven. Read the passage slowly and prayerfully. Is there one word or phrase that you feel moved to focus on?

LUKE 1:46–56
Mary said:
"My soul proclaims the greatness of the Lord;
my spirit rejoices in God my savior.
For he has looked upon his lowly servant.
From this day all generations will call me blessed:
the Almighty has done great things for me,
and holy is his Name.
He has mercy on those who fear him
in every generation.
He has shown the strength of his arm,
and has scattered the proud in their conceit.
He has cast down the mighty from their thrones
and has lifted up the lowly.

He has filled the hungry with good things,
*   and the rich he has sent away empty.*
He has come to the help of his servant Israel
*   for he remembered his promise of mercy,*
*   the promise he made to our fathers,*
*   to Abraham and his children for ever."*
Mary remained with Elizabeth about three months and
then returned to her home. (Lectionary)

Meditatio: Have you noticed news stories in which God humbled the proud or lifted up the lowly? How has God done great things for you? Have you experienced his mercy, blessing, or strength? Or perhaps you feel lowly and humbled, like someone who needs to be raised from the dust.

You are waiting for the King of all Nations to rescue you with the might of his arm. Reflect for a few minutes, perhaps focusing on a word or phrase that speaks to you. Then read the passage again slowly.

Oratio: Speak to God what is on your heart and mind: your thoughts, feelings, and desires. When you are done speaking, read the passage one more time.

Contemplatio: Open your heart to receive what God wants to give you. Maybe it is a thought, a word, or a sense of peace. God is with you in this ordinary moment. Even his challenging words come with love. Rest in and savor his love for you. Be present. Be lowly.

QUESTIONS FOR JOURNALING
1.   My favorite word or phrase was …
2.   God fulfilled his promises to me when …
3.   I rejoice in God my Savior when I recall …
4.   Mary takes Jesus with her wherever she goes. How can I take Jesus with me today?

Close with a brief conversation with God, giving thanks for your prayer experience. Then read today's Scripture one more time as a prayer of praise.

December 23 — Wednesday
Countdown to Christmas: Three

O Emmanuel, our King and Giver of Law:
come to save us, Lord our God!

Preparation: Come, Holy Spirit, enlighten the eyes of my heart.

Be present to the God who is always present to you. Call to mind his loving care for you, and spend the first minute of your prayer resting in the free, unearned gift of loving and being loved.

Set the Scene: As you read the passage, imagine Elizabeth's neighbors and relatives gathering to celebrate the birth of a healthy baby boy. The name John means "God is gracious."

LUKE 1:57–66

When the time arrived for Elizabeth to have her child she gave birth to a son. Her neighbors and relatives heard that the Lord had shown his great mercy toward her, and they rejoiced with her. When they came on the eighth day to circumcise the child, they were going to call him Zechariah after his father, but his mother said in reply, "No. He will be called John." But they answered her, "There is no one among your relatives who has this name." So they made signs, asking his father what he wished him to be called. He asked for a tablet and wrote, "John is his name," and all were amazed. Immediately his mouth was opened, his tongue freed, and he spoke blessing God. Then fear came upon all their neighbors, and all these matters were discussed throughout the hill country of Judea. All who heard these things took them to heart, saying, "What, then, will this child be?" For surely the hand of the Lord was with him.

Action! Consider the scene. Zechariah is a silent participant. Imagine the look on his face as he meets his son and welcomes his guests. Imagine the look on everyone's face when suddenly he can speak again!

Read the passage a second time. Even though Mary isn't mentioned, she was probably in the crowd somewhere, as Scripture tells us that she remained with Elizabeth "about three months" (Lk 1:56). Where are you in the crowd?

Acknowledge: Read the passage a third time, and also reread the antiphon for today.

How do you feel at the birth of John the Baptist, who will prepare the way for the King, the lawgiver, the Savior of the world? What thoughts and feelings rise to the surface?

Relate: Speak to God what is in your heart. If you have a hard time expressing yourself, maybe Zechariah can help!

Receive: Receive whatever is in God's heart for you — his thoughts, feelings, desires. Does your heavenly Father look at you as Zechariah looked at his son?

Respond: Let the Father look at you, and look back at him. Savor the joy of being your Father's child for a minute or two before moving on.

QUESTIONS FOR JOURNALING
1. I was surprised by …
2. The Father seemed to be saying to me …
3. When do I feel tongue-tied? Was there anything today that I had a hard time accepting?
4. I ended prayer wanting …

_____

_____

_____

_____

_____

_____

_____

_____

_____

_____

_____

_____

_____

_____

_____

_____

Close with a brief conversation with God, giving thanks for your prayer experience. Then pray an Our Father.

December 24 — Thursday
Countdown to Christmas: Two

O Radiant Dawn,
splendor of eternal light, sun of justice:
come and shine on those who dwell in
darkness and in the shadow of death.

Preparation: Come, Holy Spirit, enlighten the eyes of my heart.

Be present to the God who is always present to you. Call to mind his loving care for you. Spend a minute resting in the free, unearned gift of loving and being loved.

Lectio: Zechariah hasn't spoken for nine months — and now he has a lot to say! He knows that Jesus has come to set us free from a slavery far greater than that of the Israelites in Egypt or oppression by the Romans. Read this passage slowly and prayerfully. Is there a word or phrase that speaks to you most strongly?

LUKE 1:67–79

Zechariah his father, filled with the Holy Spirit, prophe-
sied, saying:
"Blessed be the Lord, the God of Israel;
  for he has come to his people and set them free.
He has raised up for us a mighty Savior,
  born of the house of his servant David.
Through his prophets he promised of old
  that he would save us from our enemies,
  from the hands of all who hate us.
He promised to show mercy to our fathers
  and to remember his holy covenant.

This was the oath he swore to our father Abraham:
  to set us free from the hand of our enemies,
  free to worship him without fear,
  holy and righteous in his sight all the days of our life.
You, my child, shall be called the prophet of the Most High,
  for you will go before the Lord to prepare his way,
  to give his people knowledge of salvation
  by the forgiveness of their sins.
  In the tender compassion of our God
  the dawn from on high shall break upon us,
  to shine on those who dwell in darkness and the
      shadow of death,
  and to guide our feet into the way of peace." (Lectionary)

Meditatio: "The dawn from on high shall break upon us." The word *Oriens* can be translated "dawn." Have you felt God's light dawning on you, shining more brightly, these last twenty-seven days? Has God been guiding your "feet into the way of peace"? Reread the passage, or maybe just the part that speaks to you.

Oratio: What do you want to say to God, with the birth of his Son so close at hand? Tell him what is on your heart and mind. When you are done, read the passage again, soaking in it.

Contemplatio: Open your heart to receive what God wants to give you. God loves every child like an only child. Rest in and savor his love for you. Let the dawn from on high shine upon you.

QUESTIONS FOR JOURNALING
1. I see more clearly after these twenty-seven days …
2. I more strongly desire …
3. I need patience as I wait for …
4. This Christmas my deepest desire is for …

_____

_____

_____

_____

_____

_____

_____

_____

_____

_____

_____

_____

_____

_____

_____

_____

_____

_____

_____

Close with a brief conversation with God, giving thanks for your prayer experience. Then read Zechariah's words one more time as a prayer of praise.

December 25 — Friday
The Nativity of Our Lord Jesus Christ

Preparation: Come, Holy Spirit, enlighten the eyes of my heart.

Be present to the God who is always present to you. Call to mind his loving care for you, and spend a minute resting in the free, unearned gift of loving and being loved.

Set the Scene: We like to think of the Nativity as something easy, peaceful, and cozy. But our Gospel implies crowds thronging to fulfill the census decree, a long journey on dusty roads with a very pregnant woman, and homelessness at the most inopportune time. Read through the Gospel to set the scene in your imagination.

LUKE 2:1–20

In those days a decree went out from Caesar Augustus that the whole world should be enrolled. This was the first enrollment, when Quirinius was governor of Syria. So all went to be enrolled, each to his own town. And Joseph too went up from Galilee from the town of Nazareth to Judea, to the city of David that is called Bethlehem, because he was of the house and family of David, to be enrolled with Mary, his betrothed, who was with child. While they were there, the time came for her to have her child, and she gave birth to her firstborn son. She wrapped him in swaddling clothes and laid him in a manger, because there was no room for them in the inn.

Now there were shepherds in that region living in the fields and keeping the night watch over their flock. The angel of the Lord appeared to them and the glory of the Lord shone around them, and they were struck with great fear. The angel said to them, "Do not be afraid; for behold, I proclaim to you good news of great joy that will be for all the people. For today in the city of David a savior has been born for you who is Messiah and Lord. And this will be a sign for you: you will find an infant wrapped in swaddling clothes and lying in a manger." And suddenly there was a multitude of the heavenly host with the angel, praising God and saying:

> *"Glory to God in the highest*
> *and on earth peace to those on whom his favor rests."*

When the angels went away from them to heaven, the shepherds said to one another, "Let us go, then, to Bethlehem to see this thing that has taken place, which the Lord has made known to us." So they went in haste and found Mary and Joseph, and the infant lying in the manger. When they saw this, they made known the message that had been told them about this child. All who heard it were amazed by what had been told them by the shepherds. And Mary kept all these things, reflecting on them in her heart. Then the shepherds returned, glorifying and praising God for all they had heard and seen, just as it had been told to them.

Action! World events collide to bring the little family to Bethlehem, to fulfill an ancient prophecy regarding the birthplace of the Messiah. God provides an unorthodox but effective bed for his little Son. God "lifts up the lowly" by inviting humble shepherds to come and adore the newborn king.

Acknowledge: Read the passage a second time, and play the scene in your mind. Where do you find yourself?

You are watching God fulfill his promise of mercy. What is in Mary's heart? Joseph's heart? The heart of the shepherds? Your heart?

Relate: Tell God what is in your heart.

Receive: Read the passage a third time. Receive whatever is in God's heart for you. Perhaps you can ask Mary to let you hold her child. What rises in your heart as you receive the Savior?

Respond: Savor the joy of holding the Son and being held by the Father for a little while.

QUESTIONS FOR JOURNALING
1. I saw God's love particularly when …
2. The glory of the Lord shone at Christmas when…
3. The Father seemed to be saying to me …
4. I was surprised by …
5. My heart rested when …

Close with a brief conversation with God about your prayer experience. Then pray an Our Father.

December 26 — Saturday
Second Day in the Octave of Christmas

The feast of Christmas is too big to fit into one day. For eight days we celebrate the long-awaited radiant Dawn, the Sun of Justice and King of all Nations who is Christ the Lord. Eat Christmas cookies! Sing Christmas carols!

The Gloria is sung at Mass for all eight days of the octave. Some of these days are special feast days dedicated to particular saints.

SAINT STEPHEN, DEACON AND MARTYR

Stephen was one of seven men chosen to be the first deacons of the infant Church (see Acts 6:1–6). He did great wonders and signs, and he preached the Gospel with such wisdom that his opponents were confounded. They falsely accused him of blasphemy, and a mob stoned him to death (Acts 6:8—8:1).

Stephen is the first in a long line of faithful servants who gave their lives in witness to the true King. This feast reminds us that Jesus was born into time so that Stephen, and all of us, could be born into eternity.

REVIEW

Preparation: Come, Holy Spirit, enlighten the eyes of my heart.

Call to mind God's loving care for you, and spend the first minute of your prayer resting in the free, unearned gift of loving and being loved.

Flip through your past week's journal entries. As you do, notice what emerged in the conversations. Here are some questions to help you:

1. Where did I notice God, and what was he doing or saying?
2. How did I respond to what God was doing?
3. I felt God's love most strongly when …
4. I found myself struggling with …
5. I'm grateful for …

_____

_____

_____

_____

_____

_____

_____

_____

_____

_____

_____

Now go back to your journal entries from the First Sunday of Advent and the first couple days of the journey.

1. What did I desire as I began this journey? Have those desires grown or changed in some way?
2. Do I notice a particular theme that has been emerging on my Advent pilgrimage?
3. Do I have recurring fears or struggles that Jesus is wanting to address with me?
4. How has this Advent journey changed me?
5. My strongest sense, image, moment, or experience of God's loving presence was …

Savor that strongest sense, image, moment, or experience of God's loving presence. Rest there for a minute or two. Then pray an Our Father.

Week Five

When to Use Each Form of Prayer

I have taught you three different forms of prayer. *Lectio divina* can be used to pray with any Scripture. Think of it as the default prayer form. Remember that the key to this prayer form is to see Scripture as a conversation starter.

Imaginative prayer works best with Scripture passages that have a lot of action in them, particularly Gospel passages. You use your imagination as the conversation starter.

Both these prayer forms transition into conversation with God. As you may have noticed last week, I am using *lectio divina,* imaginative prayer, or a combination — depending on what seems to fit the passage best. My notes are just suggestions for you. If you like one form over the other, feel free to use that. Whatever works for you!

Relational Prayer doesn't work well by itself as a form of praying with Scripture. It can form a part of imaginative prayer, as we have seen. It is also a good way to pray about everyday experiences.

Let's say a conversation with someone leaves me particularly angry and frustrated. Instead of stewing on those feelings, I can pray with them. I first **acknowledge** what I am feeling. Then I **relate** my thoughts and feelings to the Lord. Next I **receive** God's care for me and also his perspective on the troubling encounter. Then I **respond** to the Lord.

Everyday hurts are transformed into encounters with the merciful love of God. It's like magic, only better. We call it grace. Relational prayer will be part of our weekly review each Saturday.

Grace of the Week: We continue to celebrate the Octave of Christmas. Our readings will be drawn from the daily Mass readings or the Scriptures for the feast day. Pray for a deeper sense of peace and joy in the birth of Jesus, and pray that his light will shine in the dark corners of your heart and your world.

December 27 — Sunday

Third Day in the Octave of Christmas

THE HOLY FAMILY OF JESUS, MARY, AND JOSEPH

Preparation: Come, Holy Spirit, enlighten the eyes of my heart.

Be present to the God who is always present to you. Call to mind his loving care for you, and spend the first minute of your prayer resting in the free, unearned gift of loving and being loved.

Set the Scene: Jewish law considered a mother unclean for forty days after giving birth to a male child (see Lv 12:1–8). She would then offer the sacrifice of a lamb. The Holy Family was too poor to afford a lamb, so they were permitted to offer two small birds instead.

The location is the majestic and most sacred temple in Jerusalem. Saint Luke shows us that, in the person of Jesus, God himself has come to visit the temple, where he has long been worshipped. Only an old man and an old woman recognize this momentous occasion. They symbolize the longing for God in every human heart and faithful Israel grown old awaiting its Savior. They also remind us of all the elderly who faithfully worship God and trust in his promises.

LUKE 2:22–40

When the days were completed for their purification according to the law of Moses, they took him up to Jerusalem to present him to the Lord, just as it is written in the law of the Lord, Every male that opens the womb shall be consecrated to the Lord, *and to offer the sacrifice of a pair of turtledoves or two young pigeons, in accordance with the dictate in the law of the Lord.*

Now there was a man in Jerusalem whose name was Simeon. This man was righteous and devout, awaiting the consolation of Israel, and the Holy Spirit was upon him. It had been revealed to him by the Holy Spirit that he should not see death before he had seen the Christ of the Lord. He came in the Spirit into the temple; and when the parents brought in the child Jesus to perform the custom of the law in regard to him, he took him into his arms and blessed God, saying:

"Now, Master, you may let your servant go
in peace, according to your word,
for my eyes have seen your salvation,
which you prepared in sight of all the peoples,
a light for revelation to the Gentiles,
and glory for your people Israel."

The child's father and mother were amazed at what was said about him; and Simeon blessed them and said to Mary his mother, "Behold, this child is destined for the fall and rise of many in Israel, and to be a sign that will be contradicted — and you yourself a sword will pierce — so that the thoughts of many hearts may be revealed." There was also a prophetess, Anna, the daughter of Phanuel, of the tribe of Asher. She was advanced in years, having lived seven years with her husband after her marriage, and then as a widow until she was eighty-four. She never left the temple, but worshiped night and day with fasting and prayer. And coming forward at that very time, she gave thanks to God and spoke about the child to all who were awaiting the redemption of Jerusalem. When they had fulfilled all the prescriptions of the law of the Lord, they returned to Galilee, to their own town of Nazareth. The child grew and became strong, filled with wisdom; and the favor of God was upon him. (Lectionary)

Action! See the humble family and the glorious temple. See the wrinkles in the elderly faces, the love of Simeon and Anna, and their joy that God's promises are being fulfilled. What part of the passage speaks to you? Read it a second time, and allow the scene to play in your mind.

Acknowledge: Focus on the part of the reading that speaks to you. What thoughts, feelings, and desires are rising in your heart?

Relate: Speak to God what is in your heart.

Receive: Read the passage a third time. Listen to what the Holy Spirit wants to reveal to you. Will Mary let you hold the Christ Child?

Respond: Give thanks to God, and bless him in your own words.

QUESTIONS FOR JOURNALING
1. I was surprised by …
2. The passage that most spoke to me was …
3. What am I waiting for from God? Am I patient or anxious?
4. Do I desire to be filled with the Holy Spirit, as Simeon did?
5. I ended prayer wanting …

Close with a brief conversation with God, giving thanks for your prayer experience. Then repeat Simeon's words as a prayer:

> *"Now, Master, you may let your servant go*
> *in peace, according to your word,*
> *for my eyes have seen your salvation,*
> *which you prepared in sight of all the peoples,*
> *a light for revelation to the Gentiles,*
> *and glory for your people Israel."*

Fourth Day in the Octave of Christmas

THE HOLY INNOCENTS, MARTYRS

Preparation: Come, Holy Spirit, enlighten the eyes of my heart.

Be present to the God who is always present to you. Call to mind his loving care for you, and spend a minute resting in the free, unearned gift of loving and being loved.

Set the Scene: The Christmas story is not all peace and love. There is a darkness at the edges, looking to devour the Light. The foreigners were more open to God's plan than the Jewish king, who saw the true King as a threat to his kingdom. Matthew wants to remind us of Pharaoh, the great enemy of God's plans, who had all the Hebrew baby boys thrown into the Nile River (see Ex 1:22).

Tradition has painted this feast not as a senseless killing but as the lowly winning a victory over the mighty on his throne. An ancient sermon says of the Innocents, "They cannot use their limbs to engage in battle, yet already they bear off the palm of victory."

MATTHEW 2:13–18

When the magi had departed, behold, the angel of the Lord appeared to Joseph in a dream and said, "Rise, take the child and his mother, flee to Egypt, and stay there until I tell you. Herod is going to search for the child to destroy him." Joseph rose and took the child and his mother by night and departed for Egypt. He stayed there until the death of Herod, that what the Lord had said through the prophet might be fulfilled, Out of Egypt I called my son.

When Herod realized that he had been deceived by the magi, he became furious. He ordered the massacre of all the boys in Bethlehem and its vicinity two years old and under, in accordance with the time he had ascertained from the magi. Then was fulfilled what had been said through Jeremiah the prophet:

> *A voice was heard in Ramah,*
> *sobbing and loud lamentation;*
> *Rachel weeping for her children,*
> *and she would not be consoled,*
> *since they were no more. (Lectionary)*

Action! Read the passage a second time, playing the scene in your mind. Where is God's loving care in this tragedy?

Acknowledge: Read the passage a third time. What thoughts, feelings, and desires rise in your heart?

Relate: Speak to God what is in your heart. Share any burden with him. Look at him, and let him look at you.

Receive: What does God want to say to you? Or how does he lift your burden? Be open to receiving his answers.

Respond: How does God's response change your perspective? Speak to him about that. Let your relationship with him deepen.

QUESTIONS FOR JOURNALING
1. How is God's light shining in the midst of darkness?
2. What new way of thinking or responding am I being invited to?
3. In what ways have I experienced darkness, confusion, even a seemingly senseless death?
4. How has God's light shone in my darkness?
5. How is God calling me out of darkness, as he did Joseph?

Close with a brief conversation with God, giving thanks for your prayer experience. Then pray an Our Father.

December 29 — Tuesday
Fifth Day in the Octave of Christmas

SAINT THOMAS BECKET

Thomas Becket was born in London in 1118. Though a cleric of the diocese of Canterbury, he became chancellor to King Henry II and took a leading part in a military expedition against the French. When the archbishop died, Thomas was chosen as his replacement. Perhaps Henry wanted "his man" to be chief cleric in England.

However, Thomas took his new responsibilities very seriously. He began a life of penance and simplicity. He led a protracted defense of the Church's independence from the crown, which resulted in six years of exile. On this day in 1170, knights and a band of armed men slew him in his church. King Henry did public penance for this crime.

Preparation: Come, Holy Spirit, enlighten the eyes of my heart.

Be present to the God who is always present to you. Call to mind his loving care for you, and spend the first minute of your prayer resting in the free, unearned gift of loving and being loved.

Lectio: New life flows from a relationship with God. But that life must overflow into new relationships with others, my brothers and sisters. The new commandment is to "love one another. As I [Jesus] have loved you" (Jn 13:34).

As you read the following passage, notice what words or phrases strike you.

1 JOHN 2:3–11

Beloved: The way we may be sure that we know Jesus is to keep his commandments. Whoever says, "I know him," but does not keep his commandments is a liar, and the truth is not in him. But whoever keeps his word, the love of God is truly perfected in him. This is the way we may know that we are in union with him: whoever claims to abide in him ought to walk just as he walked.

Beloved, I am writing no new commandment to you but an old commandment that you had from the beginning. The old commandment is the word that you have heard. And yet I do write a new commandment to you, which holds true in him and among you, for the darkness is passing away, and the true light is already shining. Whoever says he is in the light, yet hates his brother, is still in the darkness. Whoever loves his brother remains in the light, and there is nothing in him to cause a fall. Whoever hates his brother is in darkness; he walks in darkness and does not know where he is going because the darkness has blinded his eyes. (Lectionary)

Meditatio: Union with God is the whole point of the Gospel. And union with God will lead to love for one another. When do you find loving hard?

Oratio: Read the passage again. Talk to God about this call to keep his commandments and love your brother or sister. How do you struggle? When have you experienced victory? What help do you need from God? Ask for it.

Contemplatio: Read the passage a third time. Receive what is in God's heart for you: his thoughts and feelings and desires. Spend some time experiencing more deeply God's loving presence with you and within you.

QUESTIONS FOR JOURNALING

1. The person I find hardest to love is ...
2. I find God's love growing when ...
3. These past five weeks have helped me ...
4. Communion with God feels like ...
5. I ended prayer wanting ...

Close by giving thanks to God for your prayer time today. End with an Our Father.

December 30 — Wednesday
Sixth Day in the Octave of Christmas

Preparation: Come, Holy Spirit, enlighten the eyes of my heart.

Be present to the God who is always present to you. Call to mind his loving care for you, and spend the first minute of your prayer resting in the free, unearned gift of loving and being loved.

Lectio: "The world and its enticement" describes most people's Christmas celebrations. Notice how quickly the secular Christmas seems to pass away. Saint John wants fathers, children, young men, everyone, not to love the world but to love the Father and to be loved by the Father.

As you read the passage, notice what words or phrases strike you.

1 JOHN 2:12–17

I am writing to you, children, because your sins have been forgiven for his name's sake.

I am writing to you, fathers, because you know him who is from the beginning.

I am writing to you, young men, because you have conquered the Evil One.

I write to you, children, because you know the Father.

I write to you, fathers, because you know him who is from the beginning.

I write to you, young men, because you are strong and the word of God remains in you, and you have conquered the Evil One.

Do not love the world or the things of the world. If anyone loves the world, the love of the Father is not in him. For all that is in the world, sensual lust, enticement for the eyes, and a pretentious life, is not from the Father but is from the world. Yet the world and its entice-

ment are passing away. But whoever does the will of God
remains forever. (Lectionary)

Meditatio: Is there any sensual lust, enticement of the eyes, or preten-
tiousness of life that you need to let pass away? How can you be strong
in the word of God and conquer the Evil One? Gather strength from
the love God has for you.

Oratio: Read the passage again. Turn to your Father in prayer. Ask him
to help you do his will so that you can remain with him forever. Speak
whatever thought, feeling, or desire is on your heart.

Contemplatio: As you read the passage a third time, listen to God, and
receive what is in his heart for you: his thoughts and feelings and desires.

Spend some time experiencing more deeply God's loving presence
with you and within you. Allow his strength to overcome obstacles and
free you from attachments.

QUESTIONS FOR JOURNALING

1. I used to value ... , but I find it doesn't matter to me anymore.
2. I still need to be freed from the enticement of ...
3. I conquered the Evil One when ...
4. God's love is calling me to ...

Give thanks to God for your prayer time today. End with an Our Father.

December 31 — Thursday
Seventh Day in the Octave of Christmas

Preparation: Come, Holy Spirit, enlighten the eyes of my heart.

Be present to the God who is always present to you. Call to mind his loving care for you, and spend the first minute of your prayer resting in the free gift of loving and being loved.

Lectio: Saint John uses a very strong word: "antichrist." We often associate this word with the Book of Revelation, but it does not appear there. We find it in four passages in the New Testament, all of them in Saint John's letters (see 1 Jn 2:18, 22; 4:3; 2 Jn 1:7).

John has seen many desert the Christian faith in which they were raised. Some of them now actively deny and oppose the teachings of Christianity. John calls Christians not so much to argue with others as to remain in the truth that comes from Jesus Christ.

As you read, notice what word or phrase strikes you.

1 JOHN 2:18-21

Children, it is the last hour; and just as you heard that the antichrist was coming, so now many antichrists have appeared. Thus we know this is the last hour. They went out from us, but they were not really of our number; if they had been, they would have remained with us. Their desertion shows that none of them was of our number. But you have the anointing that comes from the holy one, and you all have knowledge. I write to you not because you do not know the truth but because you do, and because every lie is alien to the truth.

Meditatio: If you know the truth, you must act on it. Many Christians believe in God's love for them but live as if God didn't love them.

Read the passage again. How would your life look different if you lived every day in the light of the Father's love for you? Are you comfortable being a child? Turn this thought over in your mind.

Oratio: We all long for the truth. Let your thoughts, feelings, and desires rise to the surface. Turn to your Father in prayer, confident that he hears your thoughts and values your desires and concerns.

Contemplatio: Read the passage a third time. Listen to God, and receive what is in his heart for you: his thoughts and feelings and desires. Is there some kind of anointing that the Holy One would like to give you today? Open your heart to receive.

QUESTIONS FOR JOURNALING
1. The word "antichrist" means to me ...
2. I have felt burdened by ...
3. I realize that I am called to ...
4. I ended prayer with a renewed sense ...

Give thanks to God for your prayer time today, and end with an Our Father.

January 1 — Friday
Eighth Day in the Octave of Christmas

THE BLESSED VIRGIN MARY, THE MOTHER OF GOD

Preparation: Come, Holy Spirit, enlighten the eyes of my heart.

Be present to the God who is always present to you. Call to mind his loving care for you, and spend the first minute of your prayer resting in the free, unearned gift of loving and being loved.

Set the Scene: This solemnity used to be known as the Circumcision of Jesus. The ritual act made a male child a member of the covenant that God had sworn with Abraham (see Gn 17:9–14; 21:4). Medieval writers saw this as the first moment of Jesus' shedding his precious blood. It was confirmation of his humanity and also of his mission as Savior and sacrifice.

Read the admittedly familiar passage to set the scene.

LUKE 2:16–21

So they went in haste and found Mary and Joseph, and the infant lying in the manger. When they saw this, they made known the message that had been told them about this child. All who heard it were amazed by what had been told them by the shepherds. And Mary kept all these things, reflecting on them in her heart. Then the shepherds returned, glorifying and praising God for all they had heard and seen, just as it had been told to them.

When eight days were completed for his circumcision, he was named Jesus, the name given him by the angel before he was conceived in the womb. (Lectionary)

Action! Read the passage a second time, and play the scene in your mind. Focus on the Mother of God. What is going through her heart? What is she keeping and pondering?

Acknowledge: Read the passage a third time. What thoughts, feelings, and desires are rising in your heart?

Relate: Talk to Mary about what is in your heart.

Receive: What does Mary want to tell you about her Son? What does she want to tell you about yourself? What is in Mary's heart for you?

Respond: Enjoy the company of the Mother of God for a few moments, and respond to what she is telling you.

QUESTIONS FOR JOURNALING
1. I was surprised by ...
2. I had a hard time accepting ...
3. My strongest thought, feeling, or desire during this prayer was ...
4. I finished prayer wanting ...

_____

_____

_____

_____

_____

_____

_____

_____

_____

_____

_____

_____

_____

_____

_____

_____

_____

Close with a brief conversation with God, giving thanks for your prayer experience. Then pray a Hail Mary.

January 2 — Saturday
Saints Basil and Gregory

These two men were schoolmates, monks, archbishops, and close friends. They grew up in Caesarea, Cappadocia (present-day Turkey). Basil became the archbishop of his hometown, Gregory of Constantinople. This was a time when the Arian heresy was at its height. Both were famous in their defense of the Trinity against the politically powerful Arians.

Gregory preached at Basil's funeral in A.D. 379. He followed his friend into eternity in 389.

REVIEW

Preparation: Come, Holy Spirit, enlighten the eyes of my heart.

Call to mind God's loving care for you. Spend a minute resting in the free, unearned gift of loving and being loved.

Flip through your past week's journal entries. Notice what emerged in the conversations. Here are some questions to help you:

1. Where did I notice God, and what was he doing or saying?
2. How did I respond to what God was doing?
3. I felt God's love most strongly when …
4. I found myself struggling with …
5. I'm grateful for …
6. This past week, my strongest sense, image, moment, or experience of God's loving presence was …

Conclude by conversing with God about your week. Acknowledge what you have been experiencing. Relate it to him. Receive what he wants to give you. Respond to him. Then savor that sense, image, moment, or experience of God's loving presence, resting with it for a minute or two. Close with an Our Father.

Week Six

Well Begun Is Half Done

Saint Ignatius encourages us to begin prayer by reflecting upon "how God our Lord looks upon us." I used to ignore his advice and just start saying my prayers. But in the course of writing this book, I settled into one consistent way of starting prayer every single day.

I have come to believe that the preparation is very important for a good prayer time. In order for a conversation to happen, two people have to be present to one another. We know how hard it is to talk to someone when they're not really paying attention to us. We know that God is always present to us, so we need to begin by being present to him.

God never stops loving us; the sun will stop shining before God stops loving you. But do you feel his love right at this instant? Maybe not. That is why it is important to use your memory. When you experience God's love, store that moment in your heart. Go back and ponder it often. And call it to mind as you begin your prayer.

The prayer preparation is all about reminding yourself that God has loved you and that God does love you. It is about disposing yourself to experience his love again today. Every prayer should begin and end with gratitude.

Congratulations on sticking with this book so far! You are now more than halfway through your pilgrimage. But there's more to come: God has much more to give you. Keep walking and find out what that is.

Grace of the Week: This week we will savor the Epiphany by stretching it out for four days. Consider blessing your home during this time (see pp. 157–158). Then we will prepare for the Solemnity of the Baptism of the Lord by opening Saint John's Gospel. Pray for the grace of a deepening sense of your identity as a beloved child of God.

January 3 — Sunday
Epiphany of the Lord Observed

Preparation: Come, Holy Spirit, enlighten the eyes of my heart.

Be present to the God who is always present to you. Call to mind his loving care for you, and spend the first minute of your prayer resting in the free, unearned gift of loving and being loved.

Lectio: The traditional date of the Epiphany is January 6, but the liturgical feast is generally transferred to the Sunday between January 2 and January 8. We will take the next few days to soak in the mystery of the Epiphany.

We start with the first reading for today's Mass. Read the passage slowly.

ISAIAH 60:1–6

Rise up in splendor, Jerusalem! Your light has come,
the glory of the Lord shines upon you.
See, darkness covers the earth,
and thick clouds cover the peoples;
but upon you the Lord shines,
and over you appears his glory.
Nations shall walk by your light,
and kings by your shining radiance.
Raise your eyes and look about;
they all gather and come to you:
your sons come from afar,
and your daughters in the arms of their nurses.

Then you shall be radiant at what you see,
your heart shall throb and overflow,
for the riches of the sea shall be emptied out before you,
the wealth of nations shall be brought to you.
Caravans of camels shall fill you,

> *dromedaries from Midian and Ephah;*
> *all from Sheba shall come*
> *bearing gold and frankincense,*
> *and proclaiming the praises of the Lord. (Lectionary)*

Meditatio: Was there a particular word, phrase, or idea that spoke to you? What does it stir in your heart? Read the passage again, or maybe just the part that speaks to you. It might help to use your imagination to picture the scene.

Oratio: God is blessing his people: light, safe return home, the wealth of nations. Read the passage again. Notice particularly the gold and frankincense.

How has God blessed you? Speak to God in your heart. Listen to his response. Have a conversation with him.

Contemplatio: Open your heart to receive what God wants to give you. He has even more riches and blessings to bestow upon you. Rest in this moment of generous love.

QUESTIONS FOR JOURNALING
1. I felt thick clouds and darkness when …
2. It seemed as if God's light was shining on me, and my heart overflowed, when …
3. This Christmas God gave me the gift of …
4. I ended prayer wanting …

Close with a brief conversation with God about your prayer experience. Then pray an Our Father.

+

Bless your home today, or plan ahead for a blessing party on January 6. Instructions are on the next page.

Blessing of the Home and Household on Epiphany

The traditional date of Epiphany is January 6, but in the United States, it is celebrated on the Sunday between January 2 and January 8. The custom of blessing homes while recalling the visit of the magi is followed in most old-world countries. The family gathers. Candles are lit. It is most appropriate to gather around the Advent wreath, in which white candles have replaced the purple ones. But other white, unscented candles may be lit if the family does not have an Advent wreath.

The leader (usually the father or mother) begins:

> Peace be with this house and with all who live here. Blessed be the name of the Lord!
> During these days of the Christmas season, we keep this feast of Epiphany, celebrating the manifestation of Christ to the magi. Today Christ is manifest to us! Today this home is a holy place.

Let us pray:

> Father, we give you special thanks on this festival of the Epiphany, for leading the magi from afar to the home of Christ, who has given light and hope to all peoples.
> By the power of the guiding spirit, may his presence be renewed in our home.

> Make it a place of human wholeness and divine holiness:
> a place of joy and laughter, a place of forgiveness and
>   peace,
> a place of prayer, service, and discipleship.

The leader takes the blessed chalk and marks the lintel (the doorframe above the door) of the main exit door of the house as follows:

20 + C + M + B + 21
(the last two digits of the current year)

The prayer below is said during the marking by another family member, such as the other parent or a child:

> Loving God, as we mark this lintel, send the angel of mercy to guard our home and repel all powers of darkness. Fill those of us living here with a love for each other, and warm us with the fullness of your presence and love.

After the lintel has been marked, the leader prays:

> Lord our God, you revealed your only begotten Son to every nation by the guidance of a star.
> Bless now this household with health, goodness of heart, gentleness, and the keeping of your law of love.
> May all who dwell here, or visit this dwelling with their presence,
> find the joy and thoughtfulness of Mary, the God-bearer, and thus praise and thank you eternally together with Jesus,
> the light of the nations, in the unity of the Holy Spirit and the Church, now and for ever.

> **All *respond*:** Amen.

All join hands and pray together the Our Father. The leader then invites all to share a sign of peace.

Other doors may be marked by family members, especially children the doors of their own bedrooms. The family may continue the celebration by sharing a special meal together.

January 4 — Monday
Monday after Epiphany

Preparation: Come, Holy Spirit, enlighten the eyes of my heart.

Be present to the God who is always present to you. Call to mind his loving care for you, and spend the first minute of your prayer resting in the free, unearned gift of loving and being loved.

Lectio: The theme of this Psalm for the Epiphany is tribute: tribute brought to a person, not just to the nation of Israel. Read the psalm slowly.

PSALM 72:1–2, 7–8, 10–11, 12–13

O God, with your judgment endow the king,
and with your justice, the king's son;
He shall govern your people with justice
and your afflicted ones with judgment. ...

Justice shall flower in his days,
and profound peace, till the moon be no more.

May he rule from sea to sea,
and from the River to the ends of the earth. ...

The kings of Tarshish and the Isles shall offer gifts;
the kings of Arabia and Seba shall bring tribute.
All kings shall pay him homage,
all nations shall serve him. ...
For he shall rescue the poor when he cries out,
and the afflicted when he has no one to help him.
He shall have pity for the lowly and the poor;
the lives of the poor he shall save.

Meditatio: What is this king like? What would it feel like to live in the kingdom that is described?

Picture Mary and Joseph praying this psalm together as they watch the sleeping baby Jesus. What questions come to their minds? What feelings stir in their hearts? What about yours? Gaze on the baby King, and then read the passage again.

Oratio: Have a conversation with your heavenly Father about the things in your heart. Then open your heart to receive what God wants to give you. Read the passage again, very slowly.

Contemplatio: Contemplate the Christ Child. Receive from the Father. Then rest in this moment of generous love.

QUESTIONS FOR JOURNALING

1. When I read about flowering justice, I think ...
2. When I hear of profound peace, I'm reminded of ...
3. Do I feel afflicted? Do I have pity on the lowly and the poor?
4. How can I bring this King tribute? I feel called to serve him by ...

Close with a brief conversation with Mary about your prayer experience.
Then pray an Our Father with her.

January 5 — Tuesday
Tuesday after Epiphany

Preparation: Come, Holy Spirit, enlighten the eyes of my heart.

Be present to the God who is always present to you. Call to mind his loving care for you, and spend the first minute of your prayer resting in the free, unearned gift of loving and being loved.

Lectio: In this second reading for the Solemnity of the Epiphany, we pick up a new theme, that of the universal kingdom. Jesus is more than just King of Israel and heir to the throne of David. He is the one true King, Lord of heaven and earth. Justice and profound peace are promised to all peoples who are willing to enter his kingdom. Read the passage slowly.

EPHESIANS 3:2–3A, 5-6

Brothers and sisters: You have heard of the stewardship of God's grace that was given to me for your benefit, namely, that the mystery was made known to me by revelation. ... It was not made known to people in other generations as it has now been revealed to his holy apostles and prophets by the Spirit: that the Gentiles are coheirs, members of the same body, and copartners in the promise in Christ Jesus through the gospel. (Lectionary)

Meditatio: Have you accepted the kingship of Jesus? How do you serve your king? How do you make him known to others, as Saint Paul did?

The ancients compared our meditating to a cow chewing its cud. Read the passage again, chewing on its words.

Oratio: Speak to God about the thoughts, feelings, and desires that arise in your heart. Then open your heart to receive what God wants to give you. Read the passage a third time.

Contemplatio: Contemplate the gift of Jesus Christ the King. Think back on yesterday's description of the kingdom, and rest in the King's peace and justice for a moment.

QUESTIONS FOR JOURNALING

1. I have experienced God's kingdom when …
2. When I hear of the body of Christ, I think of …
3. I struggle to accept …
4. Whom do I know who needs to accept the kingship of Jesus? How can I pray for them?

_____

_____

_____

_____

_____

_____

_____

_____

_____

_____

_____

_____

_____

_____

Close with a brief conversation with God, giving thanks for your prayer experience. Then pray an Our Father.

The Epiphany of the Lord

The word "Epiphany" means "manifestation." Jesus is manifest as more than just the King of the Jews but as the king of all the nations. Saint Matthew saw ancient prophecies being fulfilled by the visit of the magi, who represent the pagan nations.

The liturgical celebration of the Epiphany is transferred to Sunday, but there's no reason why we can't also celebrate on its proper day. The Eastern churches refer to this day as "Little Christmas" or "Theophany." Many cultures have special traditions associated with this feast, including parades, special foods, and gift-giving.

Preparation: Come, Holy Spirit, enlighten the eyes of my heart.

Be present to the God who is always present to you. Call to mind his loving care for you, and spend the first minute of your prayer resting in the free, unearned gift of loving and being loved.

Set the Scene: Read this passage, taking time to set the scene. What is the city of Jerusalem like? What do the magi look like? Picture the camels threading their way through the streets of Jerusalem, then Bethlehem. What does the house look like?

MATTHEW 2:1–12

When Jesus was born in Bethlehem of Judea, in the days of King Herod, behold, magi from the east arrived in Jerusalem, saying, "Where is the newborn king of the Jews? We saw his star at its rising and have come to do him homage." When King Herod heard this, he was greatly troubled, and all Jerusalem with him. Assembling all the chief priests and the scribes of the people, he inquired of them where the Messiah was to be born. They said to him, "In Bethlehem of Judea, for thus it has been written through the prophet:

'And you, Bethlehem, land of Judah,

165

> are by no means least among the rulers of Judah;
> since from you shall come a ruler,
> who is to shepherd my people Israel.'"

Then Herod called the magi secretly and ascertained from them the time of the star's appearance. He sent them to Bethlehem and said, "Go and search diligently for the child. When you have found him, bring me word, that I too may go and do him homage." After their audience with the king they set out. And behold, the star that they had seen at its rising preceded them, until it came and stopped over the place where the child was. They were overjoyed at seeing the star, and on entering the house they saw the child with Mary his mother. They prostrated themselves and did him homage. Then they opened their treasures and offered him gifts of gold, frankincense, and myrrh. And having been warned in a dream not to return to Herod, they departed for their country by another way.

Action! Read the passage a second time, and play the scene in your mind. The magi have made quite the pilgrimage. What was it like? Did they experience frustration? How did they encourage each other?

What goes through their minds and hearts as they finally arrive? They find the child with his mother. Picture the relationship between mother and child.

Acknowledge: Read the passage a third time. This is now the thirty-ninth day of our pilgrim journey. What thoughts, feelings, and desires are rising in your heart?

Relate: Share your thoughts and feelings with Mary, the Mother of God. How does she respond to you?

Receive: What does Mary want to tell you about her son? What does she want to tell you about yourself? What is in Mary's heart for you?

Respond: You have a gift to give. Open your treasures, and give the Christ Child your gift.

QUESTIONS FOR JOURNALING

1. This time I was most drawn to …
2. I was particularly moved by …
3. The gift I want to give Jesus is …
4. I have been encouraged on this journey by …
5. Whom have I encouraged on their Advent and Christmas journey?

Close with a brief conversation with God, giving thanks for your prayer experience. Then pray an Our Father.

January 7 — Thursday
Thursday after Epiphany

Preparation: Come, Holy Spirit, enlighten the eyes of my heart.

Be present to the God who is always present to you. Call to mind his loving care for you, and spend the first minute of your prayer resting in the free, unearned gift of loving and being loved.

Lectio: There is a Nativity story we haven't read yet, which is the version in Saint John's Gospel. His take on events differs significantly from the other three Gospel writers. Today and tomorrow we will see what the Beloved Disciple has to say about the Messiah's origins.

Read the passage slowly.

JOHN 1:1–9

In the beginning was the Word,
  and the Word was with God,
  and the Word was God.
He was in the beginning with God.
  All things came to be through him,
  and without him nothing came to be.
What came to be
  through him was life,
  and this life was the light of the human race;
  the light shines in the darkness,
  and the darkness has not overcome it.

A man named John was sent from God. He came for testimony, to testify to the light, so that all might believe through him. He was not the light, but came to testify to the light. The true light, which enlightens everyone, was coming into the world.

Meditatio: God's Word is intimately connected with him, yet distinct from him. He is life, and he is light. It is obvious then, from the very

168

beginning, that the enemies of the Word are death and darkness. Light serves to reveal, to "enlighten." Turn over these ideas in your mind, then read the passage again.

Oratio: You yourself have believed in the Word and have come to know him and love him. Speak your own words to the Word. Read the passage a third time.

Contemplatio: All things were made through him, and that includes you. Enter into a communion of mind and heart with the Word. Then rest in God's abiding presence for a little while.

QUESTIONS FOR JOURNALING
1. How has God's light shone in my darkness?
2. I was enlightened by …
3. I experience God's life when …
4. How am I called to bear witness to the light?

_____

_____

_____

_____

_____

_____

_____

_____

_____

_____

_____

_____

_____

_____

_____

_____

_____

_____

_____

Close with a brief conversation with God, giving thanks for your prayer experience. Then pray an Our Father.

January 8 — Friday
Friday after Epiphany

Preparation: Come, Holy Spirit, enlighten the eyes of my heart.

Be present to the God who is always present to you. Call to mind his loving care for you, and spend the first minute of your prayer resting in the free, unearned gift of loving and being loved.

Lectio: Now things get really interesting. The Word of God has been rejected by many. But to those who accept him, he shares his own status as Son of God. He is the fullness of God and the glory of God. Read the passage slowly.

JOHN 1:9–18

The true light, which enlightens everyone, was coming into the world.

He was in the world,
    and the world came to be through him,
    but the world did not know him.
He came to what was his own,
    but his own people did not accept him.

But to those who did accept him he gave power to become children of God, to those who believe in his name, who were born not by natural generation nor by human choice nor by a man's decision but of God.

And the Word became flesh
    and made his dwelling among us,
    and we saw his glory,
    the glory as of the Father's only Son,
    full of grace and truth.

John testified to him and cried out, saying, "This was he of *whom I said, 'The one who is coming after me ranks ahead of me because he existed before me.'" From his fullness we have all received, grace in place of grace, because while the law was given through Moses, grace and truth came through Jesus Christ. No one has ever seen God. The only Son, God, who is at the Father's side, has revealed him.*

Meditatio: Turn over these words in your mind. Have I faced rejection for following God? How do I feel as a child of God? How have I beheld the Father's glory in his Son? Consider these ideas as you read the passage again.

Oratio: Open your heart to the Word of God. Share what is in your heart, and receive what is in his heart. Read the passage a third time.

Contemplatio: Jesus lives, as it were, in his Father's heart. And he wants us there with him. Spend a little while abiding in God and letting God abide in you.

QUESTIONS FOR JOURNALING
1. When have I experienced being a child of God?
2. When have I rejected God's word, God's light, God's life?
3. I beheld the glory of God when …
4. The time I felt closest to God was …
5. I feel God calling me to …

Close with a brief conversation with God, giving thanks for your prayer experience. Then pray an Our Father.

January 9 — Saturday
Saturday after Epiphany

REVIEW
Preparation: Come, Holy Spirit, enlighten the eyes of my heart.

Call to mind God's loving care for you this past week, and spend the first minute of your prayer resting in the free, unearned gift of loving and being loved.

Flip through your past week's journal entries. Notice what emerged in the conversations. Here are some questions to help you:

1. Where did I notice God, and what was he doing or saying?
2. How did I respond to what God was doing?
3. I felt God's love most strongly when …
4. I found myself struggling with …
5. I'm grateful for …
6. This past week, my strongest sense, image, moment, or experience of God's loving presence was …

Conclude by conversing with God about your week. **Acknowledge** what you have been experiencing. **Relate** it to him. **Receive** what he wants to give you. **Respond** to him. Then savor that strongest sense, image, moment, or experience of God's loving presence. Rest there for a minute or two. Close with an Our Father.

Week Seven

When Does Christmas Really End?

The liturgical season of Christmas officially ends tomorrow, on the feast of the Baptism of the Lord. But for many people, Christmas is already over. You probably have neighbors who threw out their tree on Christmas Day. Christmas music has disappeared from the radio, and all the Christmas specials are over. Many families try to keep the holiday spirit through the New Year's celebration, but then it's back to work again.

Christmas seems to slowly fade into Ordinary Time. When the feast of the Baptism of the Lord rolls around, it's more like the Church catching up with the world than a proper celebration of the end of Christmas. Christmas needs a better ending.

It seems that our ancestors found a way to make Christmas last for forty days. In medieval and Tudor England, homes would be decorated with greenery such as laurel, holly, ivy, and rosemary at Christmas time. There was no rush to take it down; it decorated the house until Candlemas Eve.

Candlemas is the old English name for the feast of the Presentation, celebrated on February 2. This celebrates the day Jesus was presented in the temple (see Lk 2:22–40). The Mass for the day welcomes the Christ Child with a blessing of candles and a procession into church (see p. 255).

Even though the liturgical season of Christmas is ending, your personal celebration can continue. I encourage you to keep your Advent wreath and Nativity scene up in the spirit of the old English tradition.

Grace of the Week: Let us continue to walk forward in the light of Christ. This week we will walk with the daily Mass lectionary. Saint Mark will show us the early moments in the preaching mission of Jesus. Pray for the grace to see your Savior Jesus Christ in a new light and to hear his voice calling you to follow him.

January 10 — Sunday
Baptism of the Lord

Preparation: Come, Holy Spirit, enlighten the eyes of my heart.

Be present to the God who is always present to you. Call to mind his loving care for you, and spend the first minute of your prayer resting in the free, unearned gift of loving and being loved.

Set the Scene: John the Baptist is living in the wilderness. He eats locusts and wild honey and wears a cloak of camel's hair, with a leather belt around his waist. People are thronging to him to confess their sins and be baptized. As you read the passage, use your imagination to set the scene.

MARK 1:7–11

This is what John the Baptist proclaimed: "One mightier than I is coming after me. I am not worthy to stoop and loosen the thongs of his sandals. I have baptized you with water; he will baptize you with the Holy Spirit."

It happened in those days that Jesus came from Nazareth of Galilee and was baptized in the Jordan by John. On coming up out of the water he saw the heavens being torn open and the Spirit, like a dove, descending upon him. And a voice came from the heavens, "You are my beloved Son; with you I am well pleased." (Lectionary)

Action! Jesus appears first in a humble way, blending in with the mass of sinners on their way to baptism. Read the passage a second time, and play the scene in your mind. Picture our Savior entering the waters of baptism. What does Jesus look like? What does he see? How does Jesus feel?

Acknowledge: Read the passage a third time, putting yourself in the scene. What are you longing for or worried about as you hear John proclaim "One mightier than I"? What is in your heart as you rub shoulders with Jesus on the way to baptism? What does this passage stir within you?

Relate: As the Scripture scene comes to a close, Jesus emerges from the water. Go over to him and talk to him. Share with him what is on your heart.

Receive: How does Jesus respond? What does he want to say to you or give you? Be open to whatever God is offering: a word, thought, or feeling.

Respond: Continue the conversation for a little while. Then rest in the love God has for you, the same love that the Father has for his only begotten Son.

QUESTIONS FOR JOURNALING

1. I was surprised by ...
2. I was especially moved by ...
3. I sensed God was with me and wanted me to know ...
4. I ended prayer wanting ...

Close with a brief conversation with God about your prayer experience. Then pray the Our Father.

Monday of the First Week in Ordinary Time

Preparation: Come, Holy Spirit, enlighten the eyes of my heart.

Be present to the God who is always present to you. Call to mind his loving care for you, and spend the first minute of your prayer resting in the free, unearned gift of loving and being loved.

Set the Scene: Our liturgical cycle has returned to Ordinary Time. And it is precisely in the "ordinary time" of the work-a-day world that Jesus comes to meet his first disciples. They are not praying in church or kneeling by a stable; they are busy making a living. Open your heart to encounter Jesus in your workaday world.

As you read the passage, picture in your mind the boats, the sea, and the fishermen. Use your imagination. What time of day is it? What are the fishermen wearing?

MARK 1:14-20

After John had been arrested, Jesus came to Galilee proclaiming the Gospel of God: "This is the time of fulfillment. The Kingdom of God is at hand. Repent, and believe in the Gospel."

As he passed by the Sea of Galilee, he saw Simon and his brother Andrew casting their nets into the sea; they were fishermen. Jesus said to them, "Come after me, and I will make you fishers of men." Then they left their nets and followed him. He walked along a little farther and saw James, the son of Zebedee, and his brother John. They too were in a boat mending their nets. Then he called them. So they left their father Zebedee in the boat along with the hired men and followed him. (Lectionary)

Action! Read the passage a second time, playing the scene in your mind.

What does Jesus see in these men? What do they see in Jesus?

Acknowledge: Read the passage a third time. Have you felt Jesus calling you during our *Oriens* pilgrimage? How did he call? What did it feel like? What does this passage stir in your heart: what thoughts, desires, hopes, fears?

Relate: Sit down and talk to Jesus. Share with him what is on your heart.

Receive: How does Jesus respond to the things you share? Be open to receive whatever Jesus offers: a word, thought, or feeling.

Respond: Continue the conversation for a little while. Then rest in the love Jesus has for you, the same love that Jesus experienced from his Father at his baptism.

QUESTIONS FOR JOURNALING
1. I have felt the call to …
2. When Jesus calls me to something I feel …
3. I sensed God was with me and wanted me to know …
4. I ended prayer wanting …

Close with a brief conversation with God, giving thanks for your prayer experience. Then pray the Our Father.

Tuesday of the First Week in Ordinary Time

Preparation: Come, Holy Spirit, enlighten the eyes of my heart.

Be present to the God who is always present to you. Call to mind his loving care for you, and spend the first minute of your prayer resting in the free, unearned gift of loving and being loved.

Set the Scene: My final year in seminary, I had the privilege of making a pilgrimage to the Holy Land. We spent some time in the ruins of the city of Capernaum. The stone pavement and some of the column bases of the old synagogue are still visible today. It was a large stone building with columns all around the outside.

This was the synagogue where Jesus observed the Sabbath. Something amazing happened that day. Picture the scene as you read.

MARK 1:21–28

Jesus came to Capernaum, and on the sabbath he entered the synagogue and taught. The people were astonished at his teaching, for he taught them as one having authority and not as the scribes. In their synagogue was a man with an unclean spirit; he cried out, "What have you to do with us, Jesus of Nazareth? Have you come to destroy us? I know who you are — the Holy One of God!" Jesus rebuked him and said, "Quiet! Come out of him!" The unclean spirit convulsed him and with a loud cry came out of him. All were amazed and asked one another, "What is this? A new teaching with authority. He commands even the unclean spirits and they obey him." His fame spread everywhere throughout the whole region of Galilee. (Lectionary)

Action! It is a dramatic moment. How do the people respond?

Read the passage a second time, and find yourself in the scene. Are you among Jesus' disciples, or are you somewhere in the crowd?

Acknowledge: What does this passage stir up in your heart — what thoughts, desires, hopes, fears?

Relate: Read the passage a third time. After the crowd disperses, go find Jesus. Sit down and talk to him about what you saw and thought and felt.

Receive: How does Jesus respond to the things you share? Be open to receive whatever Jesus offers: a word, thought, or feeling.

Respond: Continue the conversation for a little while. Then rest in the love Jesus has for you, the love that never ceases to amaze.

QUESTIONS FOR JOURNALING
1. I was surprised by …
2. I have a hard time believing that …
3. Jesus most wanted to communicate with me …
4. Is there a spirit within me or around me that opposes the work of the Gospel?

Close with a brief conversation with God the Father, giving thanks for your prayer experience. Then pray one Our Father.

January 13 — Wednesday

Wednesday of the First Week in Ordinary Time

Preparation: Come, Holy Spirit, enlighten the eyes of my heart.

Be present to the God who is always present to you. Call to mind his loving care for you, and spend the first minute of your prayer resting in the free, unearned gift of loving and being loved.

Set the Scene: Read the passage, picturing the scene in your mind. The synagogue is toward the middle of town. The place identified as Simon's house sits just a few blocks away, between the synagogue and the lake. After their Sabbath worship, Jesus and a few friends head to that house for a little Sabbath brunch.

MARK 1:29–39

On leaving the synagogue Jesus entered the house of Simon and Andrew with James and John. Simon's mother-in-law lay sick with a fever. They immediately told him about her. He approached, grasped her hand, and helped her up. Then the fever left her and she waited on them.

When it was evening, after sunset, they brought to him all who were ill or possessed by demons. The whole town was gathered at the door. He cured many who were sick with various diseases, and he drove out many demons, not permitting them to speak because they knew him.

Rising very early before dawn, he left and went off to a deserted place, where he prayed. Simon and those who were with him pursued him and on finding him said, "Everyone is looking for you." He told them, "Let us go on to the nearby villages that I may preach there also. For this purpose have I come." So he went into their syn-

189

agogues, preaching and driving out demons throughout the whole of Galilee. (Lectionary)

Action! People were restricted from traveling, working, or going to the doctor on the Sabbath, which would end at sunset. What might they be thinking during the day? Read the passage a second time, letting yourself be one of "those who were with" Simon.

Acknowledge: What do you see? What do you think? What are you feeling? Read the passage a third time.

Relate: The passage ends with Jesus heading out on a preaching mission to all the surrounding towns. Walk with Jesus. Tell him what you are thinking and feeling.

Receive: After Jesus has listened to you, be silent and receive. What is in his heart for you?

Respond: Continue the conversation for a little while. Rest in the love Jesus has for you, the love you find when you go to a deserted place to pray.

QUESTIONS FOR JOURNALING
1. My favorite part of today's prayer was …
2. I was not expecting …
3. Today I saw in Jesus …
4. Today Jesus saw in me …
5. I found myself wanting more …

Close with a brief conversation with God, giving thanks for your prayer experience. Then pray the Our Father.

January 14 — Thursday

Thursday of the First Week in Ordinary Time

Preparation: Come, Holy Spirit, enlighten the eyes of my heart.

Be present to the God who is always present to you. Call to mind his loving care for you and spend the first minute of your prayer just resting in the free, unearned gift of loving and being loved.

Set the Scene: In the early stages of the gospel proclamation, Jesus does not want people talking about him. But later, after he rises from the dead, he will command his disciples to tell the whole world. Perhaps they have to experience more than just a cure before they are qualified to proclaim the Good News.

Don't focus on this as you read the passage, but rather focus on the relationship between Jesus and the leper. Picture the scene in your mind.

MARK 1:40–45

A leper came to him and kneeling down begged him and said, "If you wish, you can make me clean." Moved with pity, he stretched out his hand, touched the leper, and said to him, "I do will it. Be made clean." The leprosy left him immediately, and he was made clean. Then, warning him sternly, he dismissed him at once. Then he said to him, "See that you tell no one anything, but go, show yourself to the priest and offer for your cleansing what Moses prescribed; that will be proof for them." The man went away and began to publicize the whole matter. He spread the report abroad so that it was impossible for Jesus to enter a town openly. He remained outside in deserted places, and people kept coming to him from everywhere. (Lectionary)

Action! How does the leper look at Jesus? How does Jesus look at the leper? People were forbidden to touch lepers, to avoid infection.

Read the passage a second time, playing the scene in your mind. What does it feel like to be touched by Jesus?

Acknowledge: Where do you feel unclean? Is there an area of your life that makes you ashamed, that makes you feel unwelcome, that you are afraid to share with others? Read the passage a third time.

Relate: "If you wish, you can make me clean." Share your struggles, your shame, your fear, with Jesus. Let him see what hurts.

Receive: Let Jesus touch you where it hurts. What does the touch feel like? Are you afraid, relieved, … ? Does healing happen? Does nothing happen? Do you want to run away?

Respond: Notice what Jesus wants and what you want. Know that Jesus loves you no matter how you feel, no matter how you receive or don't receive what he is offering you.

QUESTIONS FOR JOURNALING

1. Jesus wanted me to know …
2. I fear the touch of others when …
3. I fear to touch others who …
4. Today Jesus gave me …
5. I found myself wanting more …

Close with a brief conversation with God, giving thanks for your prayer experience. Then pray an Our Father.

Friday of the First Week in Ordinary Time

Preparation: Come, Holy Spirit, enlighten the eyes of my heart.

Be present to the God who is always present to you. Call to mind his loving care for you, and spend the first minute of your prayer resting in the free, unearned gift of loving and being loved.

Set the Scene: Jesus and company have spent some time traveling around the local towns, preaching and healing. Now they have come back to the city of Capernaum. The excitement is so great that people can't even get near the house where Jesus is. Some plucky fellows are determined to get their friend to Jesus, so they climb up and pull apart the thatched roof. Picture the scene as you read.

MARK 2:1–12

When Jesus returned to Capernaum after some days, it became known that he was at home. Many gathered together so that there was no longer room for them, not even around the door, and he preached the word to them. They came bringing to him a paralytic carried by four men. Unable to get near Jesus because of the crowd, they opened up the roof above him. After they had broken through, they let down the mat on which the paralytic was lying. When Jesus saw their faith, he said to the paralytic, "Child, your sins are forgiven." Now some of the scribes were sitting there asking themselves, "Why does this man speak that way? He is blaspheming. Who but God alone can forgive sins?" Jesus immediately knew in his mind what they were thinking to themselves, so he said, "Why are you thinking such things in your hearts? Which is easier, to say to the paralytic, 'Your sins are forgiven,' or to say, 'Rise, pick up your mat and walk'? But that you may know that the Son of Man has authority to forgive sins on earth" — he said to the paralytic, "I say to you, rise, pick up your mat, and go home." He rose, picked up his mat at once, and went away in the sight of everyone. They were all astounded and glorified God, saying, "We have never seen anything like this."

Action! Read the passage a second time, and play the scene in your mind. Where are you in the scene? Are you part of Jesus' company, an excited bystander, or a skeptical scribe?

Acknowledge: Read the passage a third time. Sin destroys our relationship with God. It leads to spiritual paralysis and death. When have you felt paralyzed, powerless to move toward God? What are the thoughts, feelings, and desires that rise in your heart?

Relate: Jesus is here for you. He knows your name, even in a crowd. Spend a little time in conversation with him about this scene.

Receive: What does Jesus want to say, do, or give you? Receive it openly.

Respond: Continue the conversation. Enter more deeply into a relationship with Jesus, a friendship in which you can be together and don't have to say anything at all.

QUESTIONS FOR JOURNALING
1. My favorite part about today's passage was ...
2. I struggled with ...
3. The crowd that tries to keep me from Jesus is ...
4. Was there someone who brought me to Jesus when I couldn't bring myself? Was there someone I brought to Jesus, or is there someone I want to bring to Jesus now?
5. Now I see that Jesus ...

Close with a brief conversation with God, giving thanks for your prayer experience. Then pray an Our Father.

Saturday of the First Week in Ordinary Time

REVIEW

Preparation: Come, Holy Spirit, enlighten the eyes of my heart.

Call to mind God's loving care for you, and spend the first minute of your prayer resting in the free, unearned gift of loving and being loved.

We have spent a week with Jesus' first disciples. We have watched him teach, cast out demons, heal, forgive sins, and draw huge crowds. God has totally delivered on his promise to send a Savior.

Flip through your past week's journal entries. Notice what emerged in the conversations. Here are some questions to help you:

1. Where did I notice God, and what was he doing or saying?
2. How did I respond to what God was doing?
3. I felt God's love most strongly when ...
4. I found myself struggling with ...
5. I'm grateful for ...
6. This past week, my strongest sense, image, moment, or experience of God's loving presence was ...

Conclude by conversing with God about your week. Acknowledge what you have been experiencing. Tell him about it. Receive what he wants to give you. Respond to him. Then savor that strongest sense, image, moment, or experience of God's loving presence, resting there for a minute or two. Close with an Our Father.

Week Eight

A Sparkler Send-Off for Christmas

A couple years ago, I attended a cousin's wedding. As the reception wore on, I got tired and planned to leave. People were telling me, "The sparkler send-off is coming." I didn't know what they were talking about, and so I left.

The next day I saw a printed copy of the schedule. There, in black and white, was clearly listed: Sparkler Send-Off. It was scheduled for just fifteen minutes after I had left. The guests had all lit sparklers, and the couple had walked through the crowd on the way out to their car. The pictures on Facebook looked pretty cool. I was sorry I had missed it. At the presentation, Simeon will say,

> "My eyes have seen your salvation,
> which you prepared in sight of all the peoples,
> a light for revelation to the Gentiles." (Lk 2:30–32)

A light! That reminds us of Christmas and candles. So traditionally this feast is celebrated with a blessing and a procession of candles, giving it the old English name of Candlemas. This little feast serves as a final sparkler send-off for Christmas. You might want to plan ahead for your celebration on this day.

There are just over two weeks left in our *Oriens* journey. How will you continue your prayer once this book has finished? Flip ahead to page 263, and prayerfully consider some of my suggestions for continuing the journey.

Grace of the Week: This week we will focus on the Lamb of God. John the Baptist refers to Jesus by this title. We will not follow the lectionary for all these days but will delve into some Scriptures that flesh out the meaning of the term "Lamb of God." We will use imaginative prayer or *lectio divina*, depending on the nature of the passage.

If you live in the United States, plan to make Friday a day of penance for the dignity of human life. In any case, pray for the grace to wonder at the gift of human life and more deeply appreciate the fact that the Lamb of God would lay down his precious life for us.

January 17 — Sunday
Second Sunday in Ordinary Time

Preparation: Come, Holy Spirit, enlighten the eyes of my heart.

Be present to the God who is always present to you. Call to mind his loving care for you, and spend the first minute of your prayer resting in the free, unearned gift of loving and being loved.

Set the Scene: John the Baptist has been preparing the way for one greater than himself. His disciples are full of expectation. As you read the passage, picture the wilderness scene again. Where is Jesus staying? Use your imagination.

JOHN 1:35–42

John was standing with two of his disciples, and as he watched Jesus walk by, he said, "Behold, the Lamb of God." The two disciples heard what he said and followed Jesus. Jesus turned and saw them following him and said to them, "What are you looking for?" They said to him, "Rabbi" — which translated means Teacher — "where are you staying?" He said to them, "Come, and you will see." So they went and saw where he was staying, and they stayed with him that day. It was about four in the afternoon. Andrew, the brother of Simon Peter, was one of the two who heard John and followed Jesus. He first found his own brother Simon and told him, "We have found the Messiah" — which is translated Christ. Then he brought him to Jesus. Jesus looked at him and said, "You are Simon the son of John; you will be called Cephas" — which is translated Peter. (Lectionary)

Action! This moment was so life-changing that John (the beloved disciple) even remembers the hour of the day. Read the passage a second time, and play the scene in your mind. What is going on inside the hearts of the disciples? What do they see in Jesus? What does Jesus see when he looks at Simon?

Acknowledge: Read the passage a third time. What does this passage stir up in your heart — what thoughts, desires, hopes, fears? What do you see when you look at Jesus? What does Jesus see when he looks at you?

Relate: Have a conversation with Jesus. "What are you looking for?" Share with him what is on your heart.

Receive: How does Jesus respond? What does he want to say to you or give you? Be open to whatever God is offering.

Respond: After a little conversation, let yourself stay with the Lord a short while.

QUESTIONS FOR JOURNALING
1. I was not expecting …
2. I was especially moved by …
3. When Jesus looks at me …
4. I ended prayer wanting …

Close with a brief conversation with God, giving thanks for your prayer experience. Then pray an Our Father.

January 18 — Monday

Monday of the Second Week in Ordinary Time

Preparation: Come, Holy Spirit, enlighten the eyes of my heart.

Be present to the God who is always present to you. Call to mind his loving care for you, and spend the first minute of your prayer resting in the free, unearned gift of loving and being loved.

Set the Scene: As we consider the theme of the Lamb of God in Scripture, we depart from the lectionary and look at a very difficult scene from the Old Testament. God instructs Abraham to sacrifice his only son. This seems unthinkable to us, but human sacrifice was fairly common in the ancient world. So father and son set out on a three-day journey to a holy mountain.

GENESIS 22:1–14

God put Abraham to the test and said to him: Abraham! "Here I am!" he replied. Then God said: Take your son Isaac, your only one, whom you love, and go to the land of Moriah. There offer him up as a burnt offering on one of the heights that I will point out to you. Early the next morning Abraham saddled his donkey, took with him two of his servants and his son Isaac, and after cutting the wood for the burnt offering, set out for the place of which God had told him.

On the third day Abraham caught sight of the place from a distance. Abraham said to his servants: "Stay here with the donkey, while the boy and I go on over there. We will worship and then come back to you." So Abraham took the wood for the burnt offering and laid it on his son Isaac, while he himself carried the fire and the knife. As the two walked on together, Isaac spoke to his father Abraham. "Father!" he said. "Here I am," he re-

plied. Isaac continued, "Here are the fire and the wood, but where is the sheep for the burnt offering?" "My son," Abraham answered, "God will provide the sheep for the burnt offering." Then the two walked on together.

When they came to the place of which God had told him, Abraham built an altar there and arranged the wood on it. Next he bound his son Isaac, and put him on top of the wood on the altar. Then Abraham reached out and took the knife to slaughter his son. But the angel of the LORD called to him from heaven, "Abraham, Abraham!" "Here I am," he answered. "Do not lay your hand on the boy," said the angel. "Do not do the least thing to him. For now I know that you fear God, since you did not withhold from me your son, your only one." Abraham looked up and saw a single ram caught by its horns in the thicket. So Abraham went and took the ram and offered it up as a burnt offering in place of his son. Abraham named that place Yahweh-yireh; hence people today say, "On the mountain the LORD will provide."

Action! Read the passage a second time, and play the scene in your mind. What is going on inside Abraham? How about Isaac?

Acknowledge: "God will provide himself the lamb for the burnt offering, my son." God stops the hand of Abraham, because Jesus will take Isaac's place in carrying the wood up the mountain and becoming the sacrifice. Read the passage again. What thoughts and feelings do you experience as you imagine the scene?

Relate: Have a conversation with God. Share with him what is on your heart.

Receive: How does God the Father respond to you? How did the Father feel when his Son was led like a lamb to the slaughter and opened not his mouth?

*Respond***:** Receive what is in the Father's heart for you. Rest in his love for a little while.

QUESTIONS FOR JOURNALING

1. I had never noticed before …
2. What really struck me was …
3. I see more clearly that …
4. My heart breaks when …
5. My deepest desire is …

Close with a conversation with God, giving thanks for your prayer experience. Then pray an Our Father.

Tuesday of the Second Week in Ordinary Time

Preparation: Come, Holy Spirit, enlighten the eyes of my heart.

Be present to the God who is always present to you. Call to mind his loving care for you, and spend the first minute of your prayer resting in the free, unearned gift of loving and being loved.

Set the Scene: God has visited nine plagues upon the Egyptians, yet Pharaoh stubbornly refuses to let the people go. The final plague will be the worst of all: the death of the firstborn. Israel can escape the slaughter by sacrificing a lamb and painting its blood on their doors.

EXODUS 12:1-13

The LORD said to Moses and Aaron in the land of Egypt: This month will stand at the head of your calendar; you will reckon it the first month of the year. Tell the whole community of Israel: On the tenth of this month every family must procure for itself a lamb, one apiece for each household. If a household is too small for a lamb, it along with its nearest neighbor will procure one, and apportion the lamb's cost in proportion to the number of persons, according to what each household consumes. Your lamb must be a year-old male and without blemish. You may take it from either the sheep or the goats. You will keep it until the fourteenth day of this month, and then, with the whole community of Israel assembled, it will be slaughtered during the evening twilight. They will take some of its blood and apply it to the two doorposts and the lintel of the houses in which they eat it. They will consume its meat that same night, eating it roasted with unleavened bread and bitter herbs. Do not eat any of it raw or even boiled in water, but roasted, with its head and shanks and inner organs. You must not keep any of it beyond the morning; whatever is left over in the morning must be burned up.

This is how you are to eat it: with your loins girt, sandals on your feet and your staff in hand, you will eat it in a hurry. It is the LORD's Passover. For on this same night I will go through Egypt, striking down every firstborn in the land, human being and beast alike, and executing judgment on all the gods of Egypt — I, the LORD! But for you the blood will mark the houses where you are. Seeing the blood, I will pass over you; thereby, when I strike the land of Egypt, no destructive blow will come upon you.

Action! As you read the passage a second time, picture the people accomplishing God's will: killing the lamb, painting the blood, and eating the roasted flesh with unleavened bread and bitter herbs. What would that night have felt like?

Acknowledge: Read the passage again. Place yourself among the Chosen People. You have been a slave in Egypt your whole life. What do you experience this night?

Relate: Share with God what is on your heart. What kind of slavery have you experienced? Do you believe that God will set you free? Talk to the Father about this.

Receive: How does God the Father respond to you? What does he want to give you, or what assurances does he offer?

Respond: The Passover ritual will one day form the basis of the Last Supper and the far greater gift of the Eucharist. God's Chosen People will gather weekly to eat the flesh of the Lamb of God and drink his blood. What wondrous love is this, O my soul?

Spend a few moments receiving and savoring the love the Father has for you.

QUESTIONS FOR JOURNALING

1. I was surprised by …
2. My heart hurt when I realized …
3. I found comfort in …
4. I have a hard time believing that …
5. More than anything, I desire …

Close with a conversation with God, giving thanks for your prayer experience. Then pray an Our Father.

Wednesday of the Second Week in Ordinary Time

Preparation: Come, Holy Spirit, enlighten the eyes of my heart.

Be present to the God who is always present to you. Call to mind his loving care for you, and spend the first minute of your prayer resting in the free, unearned gift of loving and being loved.

Lectio: This is one of the Suffering Servant passages from Isaiah. It is a long passage full of rich imagery.

ISAIAH 53:1-12

Who would believe what we have heard?
To whom has the arm of the LORD been revealed?
He grew up like a sapling before him,
like a shoot from the parched earth;
He had no majestic bearing to catch our eye,
no beauty to draw us to him.
He was spurned and avoided by men,
a man of suffering, knowing pain,
Like one from whom you turn your face,
spurned, and we held him in no esteem.

Yet it was our pain that he bore,
our sufferings he endured.
We thought of him as stricken,
struck down by God and afflicted,
But he was pierced for our sins,
crushed for our iniquity.
He bore the punishment that makes us whole,
by his wounds we were healed.
We had all gone astray like sheep,
all following our own way;

But the LORD laid upon him
   the guilt of us all.

Though harshly treated, he submitted
   and did not open his mouth;
Like a lamb led to slaughter
   or a sheep silent before shearers,
   he did not open his mouth.
Seized and condemned, he was taken away.
   Who would have thought any more of his destiny?
For he was cut off from the land of the living,
   struck for the sins of his people.
He was given a grave among the wicked,
   a burial place with evildoers,
Though he had done no wrong,
   nor was deceit found in his mouth.
But it was the LORD's will to crush him with pain.
By making his life as a reparation offering,
   he shall see his offspring, shall lengthen his days,
   and the LORD's will shall be accomplished through
him.
Because of his anguish he shall see the light;
   because of his knowledge he shall be content;
My servant, the just one, shall justify the many,
   their iniquity he shall bear.
Therefore I will give him his portion among the many,
   and he shall divide the spoils with the mighty,
Because he surrendered himself to death,
   was counted among the transgressors,
Bore the sins of many,
   and interceded for the transgressors.

Meditatio: Was there a particular word, phrase, or idea that spoke to you? What does it stir in your heart? Read the passage again, pausing to reflect on whatever stands out to you. Focus on the part that speaks most to you.

Oratio: This man's life is a sacrifice, poured out for others. Though he endures many bitter agonies, they are worth it. His stripes heal us, and God rewards him for being a faithful servant. As you read this passage again, speak to God what is in your heart — your thoughts, feelings, and desires.

Contemplatio: Open your heart to receive what God wants to give you. Jesus endured the cross because he loves you and wants to make you whole. How does God want you to experience love and wholeness today? Spend some time receiving God's love and resting in it.

QUESTIONS FOR JOURNALING
1. The heaviest part of the reading was …
2. I was really struck by …
3. I had a hard time accepting …
4. I ended prayer feeling …

Close with a brief conversation with God about your prayer experience. Then pray an Our Father.*

---

* + The U.S. Bishops' "9 Days for Life" novena begins tomorrow. Learn more at www.9daysforlife.com.

January 21 — Thursday
Saint Agnes, Virgin and Martyr

Tradition holds that Agnes was a young Roman noblewoman martyred under the Emperor Diocletian around the year 304. She is one of seven women mentioned by name in the Roman Canon of the Mass (Eucharistic Prayer I). Her name comes from the Latin word *agnus*, meaning "lamb." She is often depicted holding a lamb in witness to the innocence of her youth and her virginity.

On this day in Rome, the Holy Father blesses the sheep whose wool will be woven into the pallia worn by archbishops.

Preparation: Come, Holy Spirit, enlighten the eyes of my heart.

Be present to the God who is always present to you. Call to mind his loving care for you, and spend the first minute of your prayer resting in the free, unearned gift of loving and being loved.

Lectio: The passage uses the number 144,000 as a symbolically perfect number (twelve times twelve times a thousand). The souls were marked with God's seal in Revelation 7. God's grace has kept them safe through great trials; he has not lost a single one of them. They call and inspire a great multitude to follow after them.

Undoubtedly Saint Agnes is one of these holy ones. Consider as you read, how are you called to be a lamb for the Lamb of God?

REVELATION 14:1-5

Then I looked and there was the Lamb standing on Mount Zion, and with him a hundred and forty-four thousand who had his name and his Father's name written on their foreheads. I heard a sound from heaven like the sound of rushing water or a loud peal of thunder. The sound I heard was like that of harpists playing their harps. They were singing [what seemed to be] a new hymn before the throne, before the four living creatures and the elders. No one could learn this hymn except the hundred and forty-four thousand who had been ransomed from the earth. These are they who were not defiled with women; they are virgins and these are the ones who follow the Lamb wherever he goes. They have been ransomed as the firstfruits of the human race for God and the Lamb. On their lips no deceit has been found; they are unblemished.

Meditatio: Read the passage again. Is there a particular word, phrase, or idea that speaks to you? What does it stir in your heart?

If you are to be like the Lamb of God, you will find yourself sharing in the rejection and passion of the Suffering Servant. How do you feel about that?

Oratio: Begin a conversation with God. Speak to him what is on your heart — your thoughts, feelings, fears, and desires.

Contemplatio: Read the passage a third time. Receive what is on God's heart — his thoughts and feelings and desires. Perhaps Saint Agnes wants to encourage you. Be not afraid! Spend some time receiving God's love and resting in it.

QUESTIONS FOR JOURNALING
1. I was not expecting …
2. The part of the passage that most spoke to me was …
3. My greatest fear seems to be …
4. God wanted me to know …
5. I ended prayer wanting …

Close with thanksgiving to God for your prayer experience. End with a Glory Be.

Day of Prayer for the Legal Protection of Unborn Children (USA)

In the United States of America, today is observed as a particular day of penance for violations against the dignity of the human person committed through acts of abortion, and of prayer for the full restoration of the legal guarantee to the right to life. Offer some fasting or another suitable penance today.

Preparation: Come, Holy Spirit, enlighten the eyes of my heart.

Be present to the God who is always present to you. Call to mind his loving care for you, and spend the first minute of your prayer resting in the free gift of loving and being loved.

Lectio: Jesus became like us when the Word became flesh. He shared our flesh and blood. He took our sins upon himself, carried them to Calvary, and nailed them to the cross. This refers to all of our sins, from mean words to murder. There is nothing the blood of Jesus cannot wash clean. And there is no human being alive today who is not in need of God's mercy. Keep these truths in mind as you read.

HEBREWS 2:14–18

Since the children share in blood and flesh, Jesus likewise shared in them, that through death he might destroy the one who has the power of death, that is, the Devil, and free those who through fear of death had been subject to slavery all their life. Surely he did not help angels but rather the descendants of Abraham; therefore, he had to become like his brothers and sisters in every way, that he might be a merciful and faithful high priest before God to expiate the sins of the people. Because he himself was tested through what he suffered, he is able to help those who are being tested. (Lectionary)

Meditatio: Jesus came to set us free, as the Israelites were freed by the paschal lamb. He invites us to "[wash our] robes and [make] them white in the blood of the Lamb" (Rv 7:14). Read the passage from Hebrews again, reflecting on what it cost to expiate your sins.

Oratio: Speak to the Father who loves you so much that he would sacrifice his Son for you. See what you are worth to him. Speak to the Shepherd who became a Lamb in order to set you free and is now the High Priest who intercedes for you. Share what is on your heart, and receive his merciful love.

Contemplatio: Read the passage a third time. Open your heart to receive whatever God wants to give you: mercy, joy, new life, forgiveness, peace. Spend some time receiving God's love and resting in it.

QUESTIONS FOR JOURNALING
1. God wanted to talk about …
2. I really struggled with …
3. I want to believe that …
4. God was giving me …
5. Today I want to stay focused on …

Give thanks to God for your prayer experience. End with a Glory Be.

January 23 — Saturday

Saturday of the Second Week in Ordinary Time

REVIEW

Preparation: Come, Holy Spirit, enlighten the eyes of my heart.

Call to mind God's loving care for you, and spend the first minute of your prayer resting in the free, unearned gift of loving and being loved.

God always wants to give us more! Flip through your past week's journal entries. Notice what emerged in the conversations. Here are some questions to help you:

1. Where did I notice God, and what was he doing or saying?
2. How did I respond to what God was doing?
3. I felt God's love most strongly when ...
4. I found myself struggling with ...
5. I'm grateful for ...
6. This past week, my strongest sense, image, moment, or experience of God's loving presence was ...
7. How might God be calling me to continue my prayer journey once this book ends, on February 2?

Conclude by conversing with God about your week. **Acknowledge** what you have been experiencing. **Relate** it to him. **Receive** what he wants to give you. **Respond** to him. Then savor that sense, image, moment, or experience of God's loving presence. Rest there for a minute or two. Close with an Our Father.

Week Nine

"A Light for Revelation ... and Glory"

Soon we will celebrate the solemnity of the Presentation. Let us look ahead to this momentous event, when Christ is revealed to two people watching and waiting — and to us.

Saint Luke is the only Gospel writer who records the presentation of Jesus in the temple (Lk 2:22–40). The unseen God has been worshipped in this place for centuries, though the glory of his presence departed at the exile (see Ez 10). Now, in the form of a humble babe, he will return and be acknowledged as "a light for revelation to the Gentiles, and glory for your people Israel" (Lk 2:32).

Remember, back at the beginning of Advent, how we were told to watch (Mk 13:33)? Simeon and Anna symbolize the Old Testament, grown old watching and waiting for God's promises to be fulfilled. Though their earthly eyes may be dimmed by age, God has enlightened the eyes of their hearts. They can see the One for whom all have been waiting.

Simeon and Anna perfectly symbolize what our *Oriens* pilgrimage is all about. They recognize Jesus, the light of the world. He also reveals himself to us. He calls us out of darkness to share his light.

Grace of the Week: We continue our journey by drawing from Scripture passages that touch on the themes of light and darkness. At your baptism you received the light of Christ. Pray for the light of faith to burn ever more brightly in your heart.

January 24 — Sunday
Third Sunday in Ordinary Time

Preparation: Come, Holy Spirit, enlighten the eyes of my heart.

Be present to the God who is always present to you. Call to mind his loving care for you, and spend the first minute of your prayer resting in the unearned gift of loving and being loved.

Set the Scene: Let us return to the shores of Galilee. We meditated already (January 11) with this passage of Jesus' calling of his first disciples. But in the past week, you may have noticed Jesus calling you to a deeper conversion. He is inviting you to follow him ever more closely.

Picture the sea and the fishermen as you read the passage. Use your imagination to set the scene.

MARK 1:14–20

After John had been arrested, Jesus came to Galilee proclaiming the gospel of God: "This is the time of fulfillment. The kingdom of God is at hand. Repent, and believe in the gospel."

As he passed by the Sea of Galilee, he saw Simon and his brother Andrew casting their nets into the sea; they were fishermen. Jesus said to them, "Come after me, and I will make you fishers of men." Then they abandoned their nets and followed him. He walked along a little farther and saw James, the son of Zebedee, and his brother John. They too were in a boat mending their nets. Then he called them. So they left their father Zebedee in the boat along with the hired men and followed him.

Action! The Gospel that Jesus proclaims is exactly what we have been learning about: God created the world and made human beings to be in union with him. Through the envy of the Devil, sin entered the world and divided us from God and from one another. But God prepared a Savior for us, the Word made flesh, who sacrificed himself for our sin.

Read the passage a second time, using your imagination to see Jesus reaching out to you and inviting you into a relationship with him. He wants you to follow him, to remain with him.

Acknowledge: The fishermen believe; they follow. How do you feel called? Read the passage a third time. What thoughts, feelings, and desires arise in your heart?

Relate: Respond to God's call. If you are struggling with leaving your "boats and the nets," talk to Jesus about it.

Receive: What does Jesus want to say to you? What does he want to give you? Can you open your heart to the gift of his friendship?

Respond: You cannot fulfill the mission on your own, but Jesus and Mary will help you say yes to God's call. Respond in whatever way you are able at this time.

QUESTIONS FOR JOURNALING

1. Compare this week's meditation to the one on Monday, January 11.
2. God has been giving me more ...
3. God is asking me to ...
4. My deepest desire is ...
5. I ended prayer wanting ...

_____

_____

_____

_____

_____

_____

_____

_____

_____

_____

_____

_____

_____

_____

_____

_____

_____

Close with a brief conversation, giving thanks to God for your prayer experience. Then pray an Our Father.

January 25 — Monday
Conversion of Saint Paul the Apostle

How did Saul of Tarsus, zealous Jewish student of the law and persecutor of Christians, become Paul the apostle, who would die for the Jesus he had once blasphemed?

Saul was present when Stephen was martyred, and he consented to the stoning (see Acts 7:58; 8:1). Stephen loved and prayed for those who persecuted him (7:60). Saint Paul reminds us to never despair, for the love of God can conquer even the hardest of hearts.

Preparation: Come, Holy Spirit, enlighten the eyes of my heart.

Be present to the God who is always present to you. Call to mind his loving care for you, and spend the first minute of your prayer resting in the free gift of loving and being loved.

Lectio: As you read the passage, notice how Saint Paul begins and ends with gratitude. God called him out of darkness into the light of Christ. Now he looks forward in hope to everlasting life with Christ.

1 TIMOTHY 1:12–17

I am grateful to him who has strengthened me, Christ Jesus our Lord, because he considered me trustworthy in appointing me to the ministry. I was once a blasphemer and a persecutor and an arrogant man, but I have been mercifully treated because I acted out of ignorance in my unbelief. Indeed, the grace of our Lord has been abundant, along with the faith and love that are in Christ Jesus. This saying is trustworthy and deserves full acceptance: Christ Jesus came into the world to save sinners. Of these I am the foremost. But for that reason I was mercifully treated, so that in me, as the foremost, Christ Jesus might display all his patience as an example for those who would come to believe in him for everlasting life. To the king of ages, incorruptible, invisible, the only God, honor and glory forever and ever. Amen.

Meditatio: Read the passage again. Is there a particular word, phrase, or idea that spoke to you? How has God called you out of darkness? How have you experienced faith, love, and mercy? How is he continuing to call you? Let gratitude rise in your heart.

Oratio: Begin a conversation with God. Speak to him what is on your heart — your thoughts, feelings, and desires. Do things from your past still haunt you? Bring those to Jesus, and know that his grace is abundant.

Contemplatio: Read the passage a third time. Receive what is on God's heart — his thoughts and feelings and desires. Spend some time receiving God's love and resting in it.

QUESTIONS FOR JOURNALING

1. Paul's former sins were occasions for great humility; he would not return to his former arrogance. God humbled me when …
2. God lifted me up when …
3. Above all I am grateful for …
4. I can give God glory by …
5. I ended prayer wanting …

Close by giving thanks to God for your prayer time today, and end with a Glory Be.

Saints Timothy and Titus, Bishops

Saint Timothy was the son of a pagan father and a Hebrew Christian mother, Eunice (see 2 Tm 1:5). He was a disciple of Saint Paul, and he accompanied him on his journeys. Paul consecrated him bishop of Ephesus. Saint Titus was also a friend and disciple of Paul, who ordained him bishop of Crete.

Paul wrote three pastoral letters to these two disciples. It is fitting that the day after we celebrate Paul's conversion, we celebrate the feasts of two men whom Paul mentored in the Christian life.

Preparation: Come, Holy Spirit, enlighten the eyes of my heart.

Be present to the God who is always present to you. Call to mind his loving care for you, and spend the first minute of your prayer resting in the free gift of loving and being loved.

Lectio: We are going to spend three days in Saint John's letters. To me, these passages sound like those coming from a man at the end of his life. John reflects on what he has seen and heard and proclaimed, and he wants to make sure that we get the most important parts. As you read, consider: Who has mentored you in the Faith? Whom have you mentored?

1 JOHN 1:1–4

> *What was from the beginning,*
>   *what we have heard,*
>   *what we have seen with our eyes,*
>   *what we looked upon*
>   *and touched with our hands*
>   *concerns the Word of life —*
> *for the life was made visible;*
>   *we have seen it and testify to it*
>   *and proclaim to you the eternal life*

that was with the Father and was made visible to us —
what we have seen and heard
    we proclaim now to you,
    so that you too may have fellowship with us;
    for our fellowship is with the Father
    and with his Son, Jesus Christ.
We are writing this so that our joy may be complete.

Meditatio: Read the passage again. How have you seen, looked upon, and touched the Word of life this Advent and Christmas season? How has God's love been made visible to you? Have you experienced fellowship with the Father and his Son, Jesus Christ? Compare your own life experience with that which is reflected here. Turn them over in your mind and heart.

Oratio: Begin a conversation with God. Let the things you have thought about lead you into prayer. Speak to God what is on your heart.

Contemplatio: Read the passage a third time. Receive what is on God's heart — his thoughts and feelings and desires. Spend some time resting in God's loving care for you.

QUESTIONS FOR JOURNALING

1. The Word was made visible to me when …
2. Eternal life for me means …
3. My joy feels complete when …
4. I want to proclaim to others that …
5. I want to experience more deeply …

_____

_____

_____

_____

_____

_____

_____

_____

_____

_____

_____

_____

_____

_____

_____

_____

_____

_____

Close by giving thanks to God for your prayer time today, and then end with a Glory Be.

Wednesday of the Third Week in Ordinary Time

Preparation: Come, Holy Spirit, enlighten the eyes of my heart.

Be present to the God who is always present to you. Call to mind his loving care for you, and spend the first minute of your prayer resting in the free, unearned gift of loving and being loved.

Lectio: The themes of this reading fit very well with some of the experiences on our *Oriens* pilgrimage. As you read the passage, note any words, phrases, or ideas that stand out for you.

1 JOHN 1:5–10

Now this is the message that we have heard from him and proclaim to you: God is light, and in him there is no darkness at all. If we say, "We have fellowship with him," while we continue to walk in darkness, we lie and do not act in truth. But if we walk in the light as he is in the light, then we have fellowship with one another, and the blood of his Son Jesus cleanses us from all sin. If we say, "We are without sin," we deceive ourselves, and the truth is not in us. If we acknowledge our sins, he is faithful and just and will forgive our sins and cleanse us from every wrongdoing. If we say, "We have not sinned," we make him a liar, and his word is not in us.

Meditatio: How has the light of Christ dawned in your life through this pilgrimage? What do you see more clearly now? How are you "walking in the light" and experiencing fellowship with Jesus and others? Read the passage again. Zero in on whatever speaks to you.

Oratio: Now speak to God about what speaks to you. Raise your mind and heart to God. Bask in his light. Talk to him about what you have been experiencing on the road.

Contemplatio: Read the passage a third time. Receive what is in God's heart for you: his thoughts and feelings and desires. Spend some time resting in God's loving care for you.

QUESTIONS FOR JOURNALING

1. "Let there be light," in the world and in me. When I hear those words now, I think …
2. I find God's light shines most strongly when …
3. I continue to walk in darkness when …
4. I ended prayer wanting …

Close by giving thanks to God for your prayer time today, and then say a Glory Be.

Thursday of the Third Week in Ordinary Time

SAINT THOMAS AQUINAS, DOCTOR OF THE CHURCH

Thomas was born in 1225 to minor nobility. His family intended that he become abbot of the prestigious Abbey of Monte Cassino in southern Italy. He was sent to the University of Naples for his theology studies. It was there that he encountered the Dominicans, a new mendicant order that preached the Gospel, lived in poverty, and begged for their food. Despite his family's objections, Thomas left the Benedictines to become a Dominican.

Saint Thomas Aquinas is considered one of the greatest philosophers and theologians of all time. It is a great irony that his classmates, seeing that he was big and quiet, assumed he was stupid and gave him the nickname the Dumb Ox.

Preparation: Come, Holy Spirit, enlighten the eyes of my heart.

Be present to the God who is always present to you. Call to mind his loving care for you, and spend the first minute of your prayer resting in the free gift of loving and being loved.

Lectio: The light of Christ shows us what true love looks like and what it means to be a child of God. Many people today seem to be walking in darkness, bumping into things and hurting themselves and others. We must be different, Paul tells us. We are called to live in the light as God's beloved children.

EPHESIANS 5:1–14

So be imitators of God, as beloved children, and live in love, as Christ loved us and handed himself over for us as a sacrificial offering to God for a fragrant aroma. Immorality or any impurity or greed must not even be mentioned among you, as is fitting among holy ones, no obscenity or silly or suggestive talk, which is out of place, but instead, thanksgiving. Be sure of this, that no immoral or impure or greedy person, that is, an idolater, has any inheritance in the kingdom of Christ and of God.

Let no one deceive you with empty arguments, for because of these things the wrath of God is coming upon the disobedient. So do not be associated with them. For you were once darkness, but now you are light in the Lord. Live as children of light, for light produces every kind of goodness and righteousness and truth. Try to learn what is pleasing to the Lord. Take no part in the fruitless works of darkness; rather expose them, for it is shameful even to mention the things done by them in secret; but everything exposed by the light becomes visible, for everything that becomes visible is light. Therefore, it says:

"Awake, O sleeper,
and arise from the dead,
and Christ will give you light."

Meditatio: Is Christ's light shining more brightly now than when you first began your Advent and Christmas pilgrimage? In what ways? Read the passage again. Do you feel you have "woken up" to new ways of thinking, praying, and living?

Oratio: Talk to God about what is in your heart. Start with thanksgiving for the ways he has enlightened you. How do you feel God calling you to be more a child of the light? Ask him for the help you need to share his love by your words and actions.

Contemplatio: Read the passage a third time. Receive what is in God's heart for you — his thoughts and feelings and desires. Receive whatever he wants to give you, then rest in the light of his love.

QUESTIONS FOR JOURNALING

1. I notice the darkness of the world most strongly …
2. I feel most awake and alive when …
3. These few weeks of Scripture and prayer have helped me to …
4. I ended prayer wanting …
5. I sense the Lord calling me to a new way of acting, thinking, or living …

Close by giving thanks to God for your prayer time today, and say a Glory Be.

Friday of the Third Week of Ordinary Time

Preparation: Come, Holy Spirit, enlighten the eyes of my heart.

Be present to the God who is always present to you. Call to mind his loving care for you, and spend the first minute of your prayer resting in the free, unearned gift of loving and being loved.

Lectio: In the end, love wins. God conquers the enemy, good defeats evil, and the light conquers the darkness forever and ever. God's servants shall worship him, and they shall see his face.

As you read the passage, notice what words or phrases strike you.

REVELATION 21:9–12, 22–27; 22:1–5

One of the seven angels who held the seven bowls filled with the seven last plagues came and said to me, "Come here. I will show you the bride, the wife of the Lamb." He took me in spirit to a great, high mountain and showed me the holy city Jerusalem coming down out of heaven from God. It gleamed with the splendor of God. Its radiance was like that of a precious stone, like jasper, clear as crystal. It had a massive, high wall, with twelve gates where twelve angels were stationed and on which names were inscribed, [the names] of the twelve tribes of the Israelites. ...

I saw no temple in the city, for its temple is the Lord God almighty and the Lamb. The city had no need of sun or moon to shine on it, for the glory of God gave it light, and its lamp was the Lamb. The nations will walk by its light, and to it the kings of the earth will bring their treasure. During the day its gates will never be shut, and there will be no night there. The treasure and wealth of the nations will be brought there, but nothing unclean will enter it, nor any[one] who does abominable things or tells lies. Only those will enter whose names are written in the Lamb's book of life. ...

Then the angel showed me the river of life-giving water, sparkling like crystal, flowing from the throne of God and of the Lamb down the middle of its street. On either side of the river grew the tree of life that produces fruit twelve times a year, once each month; the leaves of the trees serve as medicine for the nations. Nothing accursed will be found there anymore. The throne of God and of the Lamb will be in it, and his servants will worship him. They will look upon his face, and his name will be on their foreheads. Night will be no more, nor will they need light from lamp or sun, for the Lord God shall give them light, and they shall reign forever and ever.

Meditatio: This life is full of light and darkness. But our hearts should be full of light as we press on to the kingdom of light. Read the passage again. What thoughts, feelings, and desires rise in your heart as you read these words?

Oratio: Bring your thoughts, feelings, and desires to God. Speak to him from your heart.

Contemplatio: We will never experience the fullness of communion here on earth, but we will experience enough to glimpse what is waiting for us. Read the passage a third time. Receive what is in God's heart for you. Gaze on the Father, and let him gaze on you with love.

QUESTIONS FOR JOURNALING
1. Sometimes I struggle to believe that ...
2. My heart breaks when ...
3. I most deeply desire ...
4. God has even more to give. I ended prayer yearning for ...

Close by giving thanks to God for your prayer time today. End with a Glory Be.

January 30 — Saturday

Saturday of the Third Week in Ordinary Time

REVIEW

Preparation: Come, Holy Spirit, enlighten the eyes of my heart.

Call to mind God's loving care for you, and spend the first minute of your prayer resting in the free, unearned gift of loving and being loved.

Flip through your past week's journal entries. Notice what emerged in the conversations. Here are some questions to help you:

1. Where did I notice God, and what was he doing or saying?
2. How did I respond to what God was doing?
3. I felt God's love most strongly when ...
4. I found myself struggling with ...
5. I'm grateful for ...
6. This past week, my strongest sense, image, moment, or experience of God's loving presence was ...
7. How is God calling me to continue my journey of prayer once I have finished *Oriens*?

Conclude by conversing with God about your week. **Acknowledge** what you have been experiencing. **Relate** it to him. **Receive** what he wants to give you. **Respond** to him. Then savor that strongest sense, image, moment, or experience of God's loving presence, resting there for a minute or two. Close with an Our Father.

Week Ten

The Journey Continues

Candlemas, which we will celebrate this week, is one last Christmas feast day. Traditionally on this day, the priest blesses the church candles that will be used in the coming year. The faithful may also bring candles to be blessed that they will use in their homes. When Mass begins, the faithful are holding lit candles in their hands. The priest gives the following introduction:

> Dear brothers and sisters, forty days have passed since we celebrated the joyful feast of the Nativity of the Lord. Today is the blessed day when Jesus was presented in the Temple by Mary and Joseph. Outwardly he was fulfilling the Law, but in reality he was coming to meet his believing people. Prompted by the Holy Spirit, Simeon and Anna came to the Temple. Enlightened by the same Spirit, they recognized the Lord and confessed him with exultation. So let us also, gathered together by the Holy Spirit, proceed to the house of God to encounter Christ. There we shall find him and recognize him in the breaking of the bread, until he comes again, revealed in glory.

Then he blesses the candles:

> Let us pray. O God, source and origin of all light, who on this day showed to the just man Simeon the Light for revelation to the Gentiles, we humbly ask that, in answer to your people's prayers, you may be pleased to sanctify with your blessing ✠ these candles, which we are eager to carry in praise of your name, so that, treading the path of virtue, we may reach that light which never fails. Through Christ our Lord. Amen.

> Let us go forth in peace.

The people respond: In the name of Christ. Amen.

The candles of Candlemas remind us of those of the Advent wreath, which we lit to prepare ourselves for the coming of the Lord. God's light has continued to grow brighter. He has lit our hearts on fire with his love throughout this Christmas time. We want to burn and glow with that light and carry it to every corner of our world.

Candlemas also calls to mind the blessing and procession of palms, which will happen on Palm Sunday. Mass will again begin with a procession from the back of the church, this time to greet the Lord fully grown into his role as King and God and sacrifice. The candles of Candlemas also foreshadow those of the Easter Vigil, when we celebrate Jesus rising from the darkness of death to shed his peaceful light on humanity.

We spent the roughly four weeks of Advent preparing for Christ. Now we are spending forty days celebrating Christmas. Soon we will have forty days of Lenten fasting, followed by fifty days of Easter feasting. The Candlemas celebration calls us back to Christmas and forward to Easter.

Grace of the Week: As we prepare to see Simeon and Anna welcome the Christ Child in the temple, let us open our hearts to a visit from our King. Pray for the grace to truly welcome Christ into your heart and to make his love the center of your life.

January 31 — Sunday
Fourth Sunday in Ordinary Time

Preparation: Come, Holy Spirit, enlighten the eyes of my heart.

Be present to the God who is always present to you. Call to mind his loving care for you, and spend the first minute of your prayer resting in the free, unearned gift of loving and being loved.

Set the Scene: We meditated with this passage, the Gospel of today's Mass, on January 12. Today we will focus on the victory of the light over the darkness. Let's watch Jesus overcome the enemy's power and bring light to minds and hearts. Use your imagination to set the scene.

MARK 1:21-28

Then they came to Capernaum, and on the sabbath Jesus entered the synagogue and taught. The people were astonished at his teaching, for he taught them as one having authority and not as the scribes. In their synagogue was a man with an unclean spirit; he cried out, "What have you to do with us, Jesus of Nazareth? Have you come to destroy us? I know who you are — the Holy One of God!" Jesus rebuked him and said, "Quiet! Come out of him!" The unclean spirit convulsed him and with a loud cry came out of him. All were amazed and asked one another, "What is this? A new teaching with authority. He commands even the unclean spirits and they obey him." His fame spread everywhere throughout the whole region of Galilee. (Lectionary)

Action! Have you ever believed the lie that God is the enemy and wants to destroy your freedom, your peace, your plans? Read the passage a second time, and place yourself among the disciples of Jesus.

Acknowledge: What thoughts, feelings, and desires arise in your heart?

Are there fears and doubts coming up? Read the passage a third time.

Relate: Turn to Jesus in your heart. Speak to him of your thoughts and desires or of your fears and doubts. Let him cast out the darkness. Let his light shine upon you.

Receive: Receive the light of Christ. Bask in whatever he wants to give you.

Respond: Respond to Jesus with gratitude and a deeper conversation. Then rest for a while in his loving care for you.

QUESTIONS FOR JOURNALING
1. Read your journal for Tuesday, January 12, and compare that meditation to today's.
2. In just a couple weeks, I find myself moving to …
3. God has been giving me more …
4. I feel most deeply rooted in his love when …
5. I ended prayer wanting …

_____

_____

_____

_____

_____

_____

_____

_____

_____

_____

_____

_____

_____

_____

_____

_____

_____

_____

_____

_____

_____

Close with a brief conversation and giving thanks to God. Then pray an
Our Father.

February 1 — Monday
Monday of the Fourth Week in Ordinary Time

Preparation: Come, Holy Spirit, enlighten the eyes of my heart.

Be present to the God who is always present to you. Call to mind his loving care for you, and spend the first minute of your prayer resting in the free, unearned gift of loving and being loved.

Lectio: We will look at the first reading of tomorrow's Mass for the solemnity of the Presentation. The prophet Malachi speaks to a wayward Israel. The people have been withholding tithes and sacrificial offerings from God. They have been unfaithful to their spouses and have taken advantage of the needy. Instead of calling them to repentance, the priests tell them what they want to hear.

The people of Israel think that God is comfortably distant from them. But God promises a future reckoning. His arrival will be sudden and terrible.

MALACHI 3:1-4
Thus says the Lord GOD:
Lo, I am sending my messenger
    to prepare the way before me;
And suddenly there will come to the temple
    the LORD whom you seek,
and the messenger of the covenant whom you desire.
    Yes, he is coming, says the LORD of hosts.
But who will endure the day of his coming?
    And who can stand when he appears?
For he is like the refiner's fire,
    or like the fuller's lye.
He will sit refining and purifying silver,
    and he will purify the sons of Levi,
Refining them like gold or like silver

> *that they may offer due sacrifice to the* LORD.
> *Then the sacrifice of Judah and Jerusalem*
> *will please the* LORD,
> *as in the days of old, as in years gone by. (Lectionary)*

Meditatio: The refining of silver and gold was a fiery process. It burned away impurities so as to create pure, precious metals. Read the passage again, considering how the fire of God's love has warmed you, burned you, and purified you.

Oratio: Do you look forward to God's coming, or do you fear it? Speak to God what is in your heart — your thoughts, feelings, and desires.

Contemplatio: Read the passage a third time. Know that God is very close to you. Receive his presence and his love. Allow yourself to rest for a little while in the Father's love for you.

QUESTIONS FOR JOURNALING

1. God feels distant when …
2. I experience God closest and most present to me when …
3. I am afraid that …
4. I long for …
5. God wants to leave me with …

Close by giving thanks to God for your prayer time today, and then say an Our Father.

Feast of the Presentation of the Lord

Preparation: Come, Holy Spirit, enlighten the eyes of my heart.

Be present to the God who is always present to you. Call to mind his loving care for you, and spend the first minute of your prayer resting in the free, unearned gift of loving and being loved.

Set the Scene: The temple in Jerusalem is the largest and most impressive building most Jews have ever seen. But soon it will all be destroyed, replaced by the one perfect sacrifice and the New Covenant in the blood of Jesus. In this humble moment, God is entering his temple. Just skim this passage at the outset. It is long, and you read it before, on the solemnity of the Holy Family.

LUKE 2:22–40

When the days were completed for their purification according to the law of Moses, Mary and Joseph took Jesus up to Jerusalem to present him to the Lord, just as it is written in the law of the Lord, Every male that opens the womb shall be consecrated to the Lord, *and to offer the sacrifice of* a pair of turtledoves or two young pigeons, *in accordance with the dictate in the law of the Lord.*

Now there was a man in Jerusalem whose name was Simeon. This man was righteous and devout, awaiting the consolation of Israel, and the Holy Spirit was upon him. It had been revealed to him by the Holy Spirit that he should not see death before he had seen the Christ of the Lord. He came in the Spirit into the temple; and when the parents brought in the child Jesus to perform the custom of the law in regard to him, he took him into his arms and blessed God, saying:

> *"Now, Master, you may let your servant go*
> *in peace, according to your word,*
> *for my eyes have seen your salvation,*
> *which you prepared in sight of all the peoples:*
> *a light for revelation to the Gentiles,*
> *and glory for your people Israel."*

The child's father and mother were amazed at what was said about him; and Simeon blessed them and said to Mary his mother, "Behold, this child is destined for the fall and rise of many in Israel, and to be a sign that will be contradicted — and you yourself a sword will pierce — so that the thoughts of many hearts may be revealed." There was also a prophetess, Anna, the daughter of Phanuel, of the tribe of Asher. She was advanced in years, having lived seven years with her husband after her marriage, and then as a widow until she was eighty-four. She never left the temple, but worshiped night and day with fasting and prayer. And coming forward at that very time, she gave thanks to God and spoke about the child to all who were awaiting the redemption of Jerusalem.

When they had fulfilled all the prescriptions of the law of the Lord, they returned to Galilee, to their own town of Nazareth. The child grew and became strong, filled with wisdom; and the favor of God was upon him. (Lectionary)

Action! Read the passage again, and play the scene with your imagination. Can you see the presence of God in this humble moment? Simeon and Anna do, and they rejoice that God is fulfilling all his ancient promises.

Acknowledge: Read the passage a third time. How does your heart leap for joy? What do you feel and experience? Ask Mary to let you hold her Child.

Relate: Speak to the Christ Child, heart-to-heart. Invite him into your heart.

Receive: Open your heart to receive all that God wants to give you.

Respond: Jesus lives in the heart of every believer. Let your heart and his heart enter into a deeper communion. Let him cast out your darkness and fill you with his pure light.

QUESTIONS FOR JOURNALING

1. I was surprised by ...
2. The part that most spoke to me was ...
3. The greatest gift God has given me on this pilgrimage is ...
4. In exchange, I find God wanting me to give him ...
5. I ended prayer wanting ...

Close with a brief conversation, giving thanks to God. Then pray an Our Father.

Once a Pilgrim,
Always a Pilgrim

Pilgrimages seem to end abruptly. You plan your destination, you struggle on the road, you wonder if you'll ever get there. And suddenly you have come to the end of the road. Then it is back to your old life.

But the journey has changed you.

How have you changed during this journey? How does the world look different? What have you been able to let go of? What have you picked up that you intend to keep carrying? What are you going to do differently?

I always tell pilgrims that they need to keep walking. Our journey is not done until we come to the end of our life and enter the presence of God. Here are some suggestions for continuing your journey:

- Pray with the daily Scripture readings. You can find each day's readings at usccb.org/bible/readings/. Depending on the reading, you can use *lectio divina* or imaginative prayer. Pray each day.
- Buy a journal. You can journal using the questions that I gave you, as they apply to your daily Scripture readings. Keep notes from your time in prayer. At the end of each day, write where you saw God that day. Use ARRR to pray about your daily experiences.
- Need more help journaling? Check out the Monk Manual at monkmanual.com. This resource provides reflection space and prompts for you on a daily, weekly, and monthly basis. It helps you live life with more reflection and purpose.
- Subscribe to a monthly missal. There are many good ones to choose from. I have used *Magnificat* for years, and I find it very helpful. It includes prayer for morning and evening, the daily Mass readings, reflections, and additional prayers.

- Subscribe to my homily podcast. Learn more at Pilgrim-Priest.us.
- Our Sunday Visitor (OSV) has a number of Bible study resources. Browse their offerings at www.osvcatholic-bookstore.com/product-category/bibles-bible-studies. Consider participating in a Bible study or even leading one at your local church or in your home.
- Lent is coming soon. Start reflecting and praying about a theme for Lent and about how to live Lent more intentionally.
- Consider making a real, honest-to-goodness walking pilgrimage. My diocese hosts the Walk to Mary every year, a one-day walking pilgrimage. Learn more at walktomary.com. Check out my website for the article "A Step-by-Step Guide to Walking Pilgrimages."

Acknowledgments

Thank you to Mother Mary, the Queen of Heaven, who gave us the Savior and leads us to him. Thank you to the Shrine of Our Lady of Good Help in Champion, Wisconsin, for welcoming pilgrims as a place of prayer, peace, and hospitality.

Thank you to the Institute for Priestly Formation, where I did my thirty-day retreat and later trained as a spiritual director. In a very real way, this book is the fruit of their ministry; I am donating the royalties to their important work. Learn more at www.priestlyformation.org.

Thank you to Tim, my first partner on pilgrimage, and to Fr. Paul, Fr. Tom, my priestly fraternity group, and many other good friends in faith.

Thank you to all my fellow pilgrims, who have joined me on various walking pilgrimages. Your companionship has richly blessed and encouraged me.

Thank you to the good people of Holy Trinity, St. Anthony, and St. Patrick parishes. You gave me some of the hardest yet most rewarding years of my life. You were patient with me and taught me how to be a pastor. You will always have a special place in my heart.

Thank you to the priests and people of the Diocese of Green Bay, in particular published authors Fr. Edward Looney and Julianne Stanz, who inspired and encouraged me to see this project through.

Thank you to my loving family — especially my parents, Jim and Marion, who often tell me they love me and are proud of me. You were my first teachers in the ways of faith, and you taught by example.

And thank you, my fellow *Oriens* pilgrim. I wrote this book for you. I hope we meet someday, in this life or the next.

The best is yet to come!

About the Author

Fr. Joel Sember was ordained a priest in 2007 for the Diocese of Green Bay, Wisconsin. He has extensive experience as a parish priest and served two years in campus ministry. He made a thirty-day Ignatian silent retreat and later completed the Spiritual Direction Training Program through the Institute for Priestly Formation in Omaha, Nebraska. He holds a B.A. in philosophy and Catholic studies from the University of St. Thomas, a bachelor's in sacred theology from the Pontifical Gregorian University, and a license in sacred theology from the Pontifical University Santa Croce in Rome. He has completed a dozen walking pilgrimages. He currently serves as pastor of three parishes in rural northeastern Wisconsin.

Between ministry and parish meetings, Fr. Joel rides a motorcycle and paddles a kayak around great Wisconsin lakes. You can listen to his homily podcast every Sunday at PilgrimPriest.us.